# CONVOY

# CONVOY

## MERCHANT SAILORS AT WAR 1939-1945

**PHILIP KAPLAN**
**JACK CURRIE**

**NAVAL INSTITUTE PRESS**
ANNAPOLIS, MARYLAND

For two good men who passed away in nineteen-ninety-six,
Joe Kaplan and Jack Currie

First published in 1998 by Aurum Press Ltd.,
25 Bedford Avenue  London WC1B 3AT

Published and distributed in the United States of America and Canada by the
Naval Institute Press, 118 Maryland Avenue, Annapolis, MD 21402-5035

Library of Congress Catalog Card Number: 97-76331

ISBN 1 55750 137 8

This edition is authorized for sale only in the United States, its territories and
possessions, and Canada

Printed and bound in Singapore by Imago using acid-free paper

# CONTENTS

MERCHANTMEN

WHEN ADMIRAL Horatio Nelson defeated Napoleon's Franco-Spanish fleet off Cape Trafalgar on 21st October 1805, only to die in his hour of triumph, the population of the British Islands, mourning the hero while rejoicing in the victory, numbered approximately sixteen million. They were a proud and almost self-sufficient people, needing little more than such luxuries as silks, tobacco, tea and coffee to satisfy their wants from overseas. Nearly one hundred and thirty-four years later, when World War II began, there were more than fifty million mouths to feed, and Britain had become increasingly reliant on a constant flow of imports, not only to maintain her position as a major manufacturing nation, but merely to survive.

Whether it was ever pedantically correct to give the title "Merchant Navy" to Britain's trading fleet can probably be questioned. There had been a time when the same ships were used for fighting and for trading, but those days had passed with the cannon and the cutlass. The fighting ships, their officers and men, remained in the service of the Crown, ever ready to wage the nation's wars, while the rest sailed the oceans of the world with one main objective—to enrich the ship-owners. And the owners were a very diverse group, with their offices in all the major ports, with a wide variety of vessels, embracing *Saucy Sue* of Yarmouth and the *Queen Elizabeth*, with motives ranging from the frankly mercenary to the idealistic, and with their employees' wages varying between the handsome and the barest of subsistence levels.

So the Red Ensign flew above a multitude of

The happiest hour a sailor sees / Is when he's down At an island town / With his Nancy on his knees, yo ho! And his arm around her waist!
—from *The Mikado* by W. S. Gilbert

Being in a ship is being in a jail, with the chance of being drowned.
—Samuel Johnson

below: *Royal Navy frigate escorting merchantmen in the Western Approaches circa 1790* by E.D. Walker

below: A convoy conference being held at Admiralty House, Halifax, Nova Scotia. These meetings were normally attended by the captain and wireless officer of each ship to sail in the convoy.

ships, belonging to a lot of individuals, each with different notions of how to run a shipping business. Nevertheless, it was due to their industry, by whatever means and for whatever motives, that by the 1930s the British Empire and the Commonwealth had developed into the greatest trading community the world had ever seen, with global port facilities and a merchant fleet of approximately 6,700 vessels—more than double the number of their nearest rival, the United States of America. It was said that, on any one day in the year, 2,500 vessels registered in Britain, were at sea or working in a port, somewhere in the world. But Britain's

dependence on the imports carried by those ships was her greatest weakness in wartime, when her long-established freedom of the sea was challenged by a foreign power. That weakness had been ominously demonstrated during World War I, when the U-boats of the Kaiser's Navy had targeted Britain's cargo ships, and there had been times in 1917 when starvation had stared her people in the face.

With that vulnerability in mind, the Government requisitioned all shipping at the start of World War II. In service, the ships remained under the management of the line owners, who acted as agents for the Ministry of Supply, and later for the

Ministry of War Transport, which, on 1st May 1941, was formed from the Ministries of Transport and of Shipping. Experts from the shipping lines, with civil servants from the Ministries, formed a central planning group which, for the duration of the war, was to decide where the ships would sail and what cargoes they would carry. The owners remained responsible for maintaining and provisioning their ships, while the newly-formed Merchant Navy Pool assumed the task of crewing.

From 1939 to 1945, the names of ships built in British shipyards for the Government, old World War I vessels purchased from the United States, or captured tonnage, took the prefix "Empire", *Empire Byron*, for example, *Empire Chaucer* and *Empire Starlight*, while those built in Canada were "Fort" or "Park" (suffix) (*Fort Brunswick*, *Avondale Park*). The Canadian-built ships were owned by the Canadian government and manned by Canadian seafarers. Some did come under the British flag and were renamed with a "Fort" prefix. American-built ships were "Ocean", as in *Ocean Vengeance*, or, if they were to be manned by British crews, "Sam" boats, as in *Sampep* and *Samholt*, and were emergency-built Liberty ships that were bareboat-chartered to the British government and renamed. The "Sam" was popularly taken to be a reference to "Uncle Sam", but the official interpretation was that it described the profile of the ship—"Superstructure aft of midships".

At any period of time in World War II, there might have been a dozen convoys on the wide Atlantic, each numbering anything between ten and over a hundred ships, some bound for Britain with their vital cargoes, others sailing outbound in ballast to collect the next consignment. The commercial fleets were composed of many varieties of ship—fast and slow, large and small, old and new, coal-fired and oil-fired—and the ships were crewed by men of widely different nationalities and faiths, some of whom felt loyalties which lay more with their calling and their shipmates than with their owners or the British Crown.

The merchant ship captains, or masters, were accustomed to taking orders only from their owners, and not from officers of the Royal Navy, nor of the Reserve, no matter how much gold braid they might wear on their sleeves. In the first few months of war, few were in favour of the convoy system, and preferred to make their way alone. In this they were at one with their owners, who regarded the days spent in assembling the convoys and attending Commodore's conferences as so much unproductive time. The masters, for their part, did not care for the discipline required. They mistrusted (and not without reason) the rendezvous in mid-Atlantic when they were supposed to exchange escorts with a convoy coming west, and they feared the dangers of collision in the fogs that were common, at all times of the year, off the coast of Nova Scotia. It was only later, when the U-boat wolfpacks began to make their deadly presence felt, that most owners and masters accepted the fact that they had to have protection, and that ships sailing alone could not be protected.

Although they were as diverse in their ways and opinions as any other group of men in skilled occupations, the masters had it in common that, like their crewmen, they took pride in their calling; they also tended to believe in a destiny that shaped all human ends, and to accept whatever blows of fate, and particularly of nature, that might come along.

Until June 1940, many merchant ships were employed in the transport of the British Expeditionary Force, with all its weapons, vehicles and equipment, to the western coast of France, and in maintaining its supplies. It is remarkable that, in the nine months of the operation, only one ship was lost, and that was due to misadventure, not to action by the enemy.

Then, in May 1940, came the Blitzkrieg—the

Before any convoy sets out, the captains of the merchantmen have a conference, during the course of which the Senior Officer of the escort makes a brief speech in addition to giving instructions as to the evasive tactics. These speeches vary, but here is a typical one—typical except for the fact that the crime of straggling is not as emphasised as usual, nor is there any reference to the other sin of bad stoking, which causes the ships' funnels to belch smoke and thus give away their position to enemy aircraft. "I imagine that while in convoy the movements and stationing of your escort sometimes forms a subject for speculation amongst you. Some of you perhaps feel that your ship is left exposed more to attack than is your fair share—others may consider that the escort is kept too far away. I know I should feel very critical myself if I were in your place; so perhaps it would be of interest to you if I explained the lines on which we work. It must be obvious to you that different forms of attack need different counter-measures. There is the U-boat attack by day, air attack and U-boat attack by night. One cannot be strong against all forms of attack at once without a very large number of escorts. For an anti-

top and above: Peter Wakker, former engineer, SS *Triton*

submarine screen, one wants to be some distance from the convoy so that a suspected contact with a submarine can be investigated in plenty of time. If on the other hand warning of enemy aircraft is received, or if we are in an area where air attack is more likely than submarine attack, the escorts will close in so as to bring as much gunfire as possible to bear on any low-flying aircraft. The problem of night defence is again a

lightning strike by the Wehrmacht, spearheaded by the Luftwaffe, on Belgium, Luxembourg, the Netherlands and France. Soon, every ship that could be mustered was needed to evacuate the bulk of the BEF, along with many French soldiers, from the beaches of Dunkirk, and to bring detachments home from Calais, Brest, Saint Nazaire, Le Havre and Boulogne. On 17th June, the Cunarder *Lancastria*, which a week earlier had taken part in the withdrawal from Norway, was ready to sail from Saint Nazaire with approximately 5,300 servicemen aboard, including a large RAF contingent, when she was hit by bombs from a Dornier Do-17, and went down. There were only enough lifeboats and rafts for a fraction of the complement, and despite all rescue efforts by the destroyer HMS *Highlander*, HM trawler *Cambridgeshire* and other ships, during the continued air attack, 2,833 of *Lancastria*'s crew and passengers were lost.

The day following the *Lancastria* disaster, the Blue Star liner *Arandora Star*, which had also been involved in the Norway operation, and had been plying to-and-fro between France and England with a weary crew ever since, sailed from Liverpool for St. John's, Newfoundland, carrying 1,213 German and Italian internees, 86 German POWs, a military guard 200 strong, and a crew of 174. She was sailing on a zig-zag course, as was customary when a ship was not escorted, off the north-west coast of Ireland shortly before dawn on 2nd July when she was hit by a torpedo launched from Kapitänleutnant Günther Prien's *U47*. The *Arandora Star* went down with 750 of her passengers, her Captain, 12 officers and 42 members of her crew.

The so-called "phoney" war, which, for the men of the Royal and Merchant Navies, had never been anything but in deadly earnest, was over, and now its reality was clear to all the world. Materially and physically supported by her Commonwealth and Empire, and morally at least by the majority of

Americans, Britain was left to carry on the fight against a rampant Germany, now joined by an opportunist Italy, and with access to captured bases stretching from Norway to the Spanish border. In July 1940, two outward bound convoys, CW 7 and CW 8, were attacked in the English Channel by E-boats (German Motor torpedo-boats) and bombers. In that month, forty Allied cargo ships were sunk by air attack alone. The ports of Dover, Weymouth, Portland, Plymouth, Falmouth and Cardiff were all heavily bombed, and inbound vessels had to be re-routed to the Bristol Channel, the Mersey and the Clyde. Nor were they immune there from the Luftwaffe's attentions.

It was decided that the headquarters of the C.-in-C. Western Approaches Command, from which the shipping routes to Britain around the north and south of Ireland were controlled, should move from Plymouth to Derby House in Liverpool, where Winston Churchill, when he was First Lord of the Admiralty, had foresightedly required a bomb-proof operations centre to be built. The "Dungeon", as it was known, was staffed by hundreds of communications and cryptographic experts, many of them members of the Women's Royal Naval Service, all working an 84-hour week, and it was from there that Admiral Sir Percy Noble, and his successor Admiral Sir Max Horton, directed the Battle of the Atlantic.

The losses incurred by the Royal and Merchant Navies in the first year of the war included a battleship, an aircraft carrier, five cruisers, three destroyers, two submarines and 438 merchantmen, all at a cost to the enemy of twenty-eight U-boats. Then, in September 1940, the major docks in the Pool of London, the East India, the Royal Victoria, the King George V and the Royal Albert, suffered forty bombing raids, in the course of which one ship, the *Minnie De Larrinaga*, was sunk and eighteen damaged, in addition to the destruction of installations and equipment, and to civilian casualties throughout the dockland area. On 9th of the month, only one ship of five in the Victoria Docks remained afloat. Of the four ships sunk there, all were eventually raised and returned to service.

These figures were severe enough, but worse were to come. From the beginning of March to the end of May 1941, 142 merchant ships, 99 of which were British, were sunk by U-boats, 179 by aircraft, 44 by surface ships and 33 by mines. The tonnage lost in those three months exceeded the existing rate of British ship production by 3 to 1, and the combined British and American production by 2 to 1. It was not until August 1942 that the combined ship production of the Allies at first balanced the losses, and then began to exceed it as month followed month.

In wartime, ships were often required to carry cargoes for which they were not built, over oceans they were never meant to sail. Willy-nilly, they travelled to and from Halifax and Liverpool, Cape Breton Island and Glasgow, Freetown and Valetta, Suez and Tobruk, Algiers and Casablanca, Reykjavik and Murmansk, Rangoon and Singapore. Often, it seemed to the seamen that their routes were selected out of sheer perversity, as though with the intention of keeping them in danger on the high seas for as long as possible. They had no way of knowing the reason for the doglegs, diversions and re-routings that were ordered by their escort commanders or Convoy Commodores, for they had no access to what was known in London and in Liverpool about the wolfpacks' movements. That was top secret information, classified as Ultra, which came from Bletchley Park, where the Government's scientists had succeeded in deciphering the German Navy's supposedly unbreakable Enigma wireless codes.

The Convoy Commodores were all volunteers, taken from the list of retired Flag Officers of the Royal Naval Reserve. Many were over the age of

sixty, and several were closer to seventy. Their American counterparts were usually Captains in the US Naval Reserve with some mercantile experience. At sea, the Commodore did not actually command the ship he sailed in, which was known as "The Commodore" and identified by a white flag with a blue St. George's Cross. He was responsible for alterations of the convoy's speed and course, and for close liaison with the commander of the naval escort, whose responsibility was for "the safe and timely arrival of the convoy". Normally, the Commodore had his own small signals staff, who remained with him on whichever ship he flew his flag. Twenty-one of these highly-respected, dedicated officers gave their lives in the course of World War II.

Any merchant ship which assembled in a convoy was covered by government insurance, and some were not as seaworthy as they should have been. Rear Admiral Sir Kenelm Creighton took a harsh view of certain British ship-owners, who did not scruple to send men to face the perils of the North Atlantic and the onslaught of the enemy in, as he wrote, "ships that were not fit to be anywhere but in a breaker's yard". A veteran Convoy Commodore, Sir Kenelm had a right to his opinion: he had flown his flag in the cargo passenger ship *Avoceta* when HG73 sailed for Britain from Gibraltar on 17th September 1941 with 25 merchantmen, an escort comprising a destroyer, two sloops, eight corvettes and HMS *Springbank*, a requisitioned merchant ship designated as an Auxiliary Catapult Fighter ship, carrying two Fairey Fulmar fighter aircraft on her launch deck. A pair of Italian submarines made the first contact west of Cape Finisterre, but the damage was done by three U-boats, which, in the following five days, sank nine of the merchantmen, including *Avoceta*. The Commodore, the master and six of the crew were rescued from a life raft by the corvette HMS *Periwinkle*. On 27th September, west of Ireland, the *Springbank*, whose fighters

different one, as submarines usually attack on the surface during dark hours. I won't go into this question very fully on this occasion, as while we are with you there will be, practically speaking, no real darkness. All I will say is that if by reason of heavy clouds or rain, we do get a few hours of real darkness and an attack develops, do not be alarmed by flares that you see. These may be star shells fired by the escort to illuminate a submarine on the surface. If the contact is good, the escort will probably drop a pattern of charges. In this case your

Aerial view of the Bedford Basin and approach to Halifax harbour. The basin was the assembly point for the great Halifax convoys of WWII. The harbour was referred to by Rear Admiral S.S. Bonham-Carter, RN, as "probably the most important port in the world."

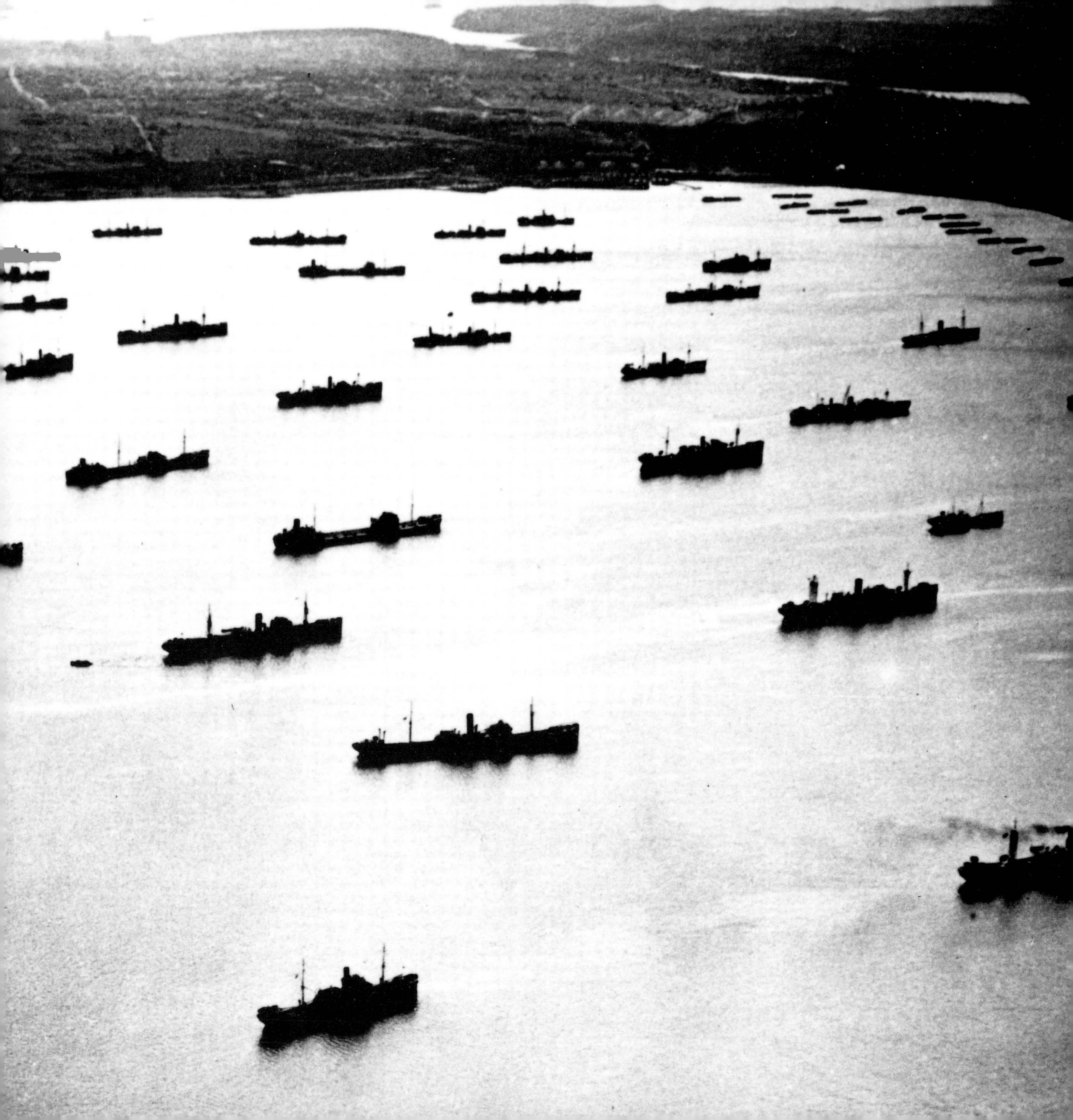

had previously repelled the attacks of two Focke-Wulf Condors, was sunk by *U201*.

To provide some air protection in the "Atlantic Gap" where shore-based aircraft could not reach (until the advent of very long-range aircraft), a number of oil tankers and grain-carriers were fitted out with plywood flight decks, from which it was possible to operate four aircraft, while still carrying cargo below. The more conventional escort carriers carried more aircraft—usually from fifteen to twenty—with the necessary communications for their control, but at the expense of any other cargo.

At twilight on 12th September 1942, the Cunard White Star liner *Laconia*, of 19,695 gross tons, was some 200 miles off the Grain Coast of West Africa, sailing unescorted for England from Suez on the 12,000 mile voyage round the Cape, with 3,251 aboard, including 1,793 Italian POWs, when she was torpedoed and sunk by the Type IXC U-boat *U156*. As the U-boat moved among the lifeboats and the swimmers in the water, the commander, Werner Hartenstein, heard Italian survivors crying for help. Signalling for assistance, he somehow contrived to take nearly 200 survivors on board the *U156*, while three other submarines, German and Italian, picked up many more. It is worthy of note that Admiral Dönitz, in his memoirs, claimed the rescue of 800 British passengers and crew, and 450 Italians, whereas British sources gave the total of survivors, including those rescued by the Vichy French cruiser *Gloire* and taken to Casablanca, and the few who survived for four weeks in lifeboats, as 975. Captain Sharp, who went down with his ship, had been master of *Lancastria* when she was sunk in the English Channel in June 1940.

The rescue operation continued for three days, but it was halted during the morning of 16th September by the intervention of an American Liberator, flying from Ascension Island, followed by two more, which dropped several bombs upon the scene, one of which caused damage to *U156*.

The episode prompted Dönitz to forbid his U-boat commanders in future to attempt the rescue of the crews of sunken ships. "This applies equally," his order continued, "to the picking up of men in the water and putting them aboard a lifeboat, to the righting of capsized lifeboats and to the supply of food and water. Such activities are a contradiction of the primary object of war, namely, the destruction of enemy ships and their crews." At the post-war Nuremberg Tribunal, Dönitz successfully defended himself against the charge, argued by the British Prosecutor, that this order had contravened the rules of war.

The war at sea went on, as bitterly as ever. Between 1st August 1942 and 21st May 1943, total Allied shipping losses in the Atlantic amounted to 3,760,722 gross tons, of which nearly 2,000,000 tons were British. Gradually, however, the tide was turning in the Allies favour and, as it transpired, May was the crucial month. It was then that the latest radar sets on Allied ships and aircraft, the new and more effective depth charges, and above all the work of the Bletchley Park code-breakers, were brought together, first to challenge, and at last to beat Die Rudeltaktik.

The month, however, had not started well. When Grossadmiral Karl Dönitz ordered 41 U-boats to attack a large west-bound Allied convoy, ONS5, the order was intercepted by the British and the escort reinforced, but bad weather grounded the long-range Liberators, and thirteen merchant ships were sunk for the loss of two U-boats. It looked like another victory for the U-boats. Then a fog rolled across the North Atlantic, the sea became smoother, and the escort's radar came into its own. Raider after raider was steadily tracked down, depth-charged and sunk, or forced to the surface to face the escorts' guns. The wolfpack retreated, and suddenly the tables had been turned. By 17th May, 23 U-boats had gone down since the beginning of the month, and there was worse to come: of 21 U-boats sent to intercept

both left: Nursing sister Vera Dunnett was returning to England from her post in Nigeria in 1942 when her ship was torpedoed and sunk. Those in her lifeboat were rescued by the corvette *Woodruff*. She is now an honorary member of the Flower Class Corvette Association.

a big east-bound convoy, SC130, only ten sighted it and only one got close enough to deliver an attack—unsuccessfully. Two were sunk by Liberators based on Iceland and three by escort ships. One of those who died was Leutnant zur See Peter Dönitz, the Admiral's own son.

It had been a long and dreadful battle, and it was by no means over. There would be longer-range U-boats, faster under water, capable of recharging their batteries while submerged, but Dönitz had seen the writing on the wall, and he stated the position succinctly: "We have lost the Battle of the Atlantic".

The naval contribution to the Normandy invasion, code-named Operation Neptune, had been in the planning since 1942 and, as D-Day approached, the Merchant Navy was more and more involved. Between January and June 1944, a million US Army personnel were carried across the Atlantic, mostly in British troopships, which included the great Cunarders *Queen Mary* and *Queen Elizabeth*, sailing independently and each carrying some 12,000 troops or more on every voyage.

Thirteen American turbine-powered cargo ships were re-fitted in Los Angeles as Landing Ships Infantry Large, and ferried to Britain by Merchant Navy crews. Forty-six vessels, also built in California as "Landing Ships Infantry", were armed with Oerlikons, a Bofors and a 4.7 inch gun fore and aft. Carrying 1,500 soldiers on their decks, accompanied by echelons of Royal Navy "Landing

(a) Keep your guns manned and fingers on the trigger. (b) Do not straggle. We cannot give you any protection if you drop astern.
—from *Life Line* by Charles Graves

far left: Seaman's memorial at Halifax. above: The ship's telegraph of corvette HMCS *Sackville*.

far right: Looking
forward from the
bridge of an Allied
merchant ship in a
Malta convoy, 21st
August 1942.

Craft Assault" on either beam, the LSIs were to form the spearhead of the invasion force. Another fleet of merchantmen, including thirty-two American and twenty-eight British ships, would be filled with concrete and sunk to act as breakwaters and anti-aircraft gun platforms off the invasion beaches, while others, with prefabricated pier-heads and concrete caissons towed by tugs across the English Channel, would form the basic structure of the "Mulberry" harbours.

The high-level meetings were over, the great decisions made, the sealed orders opened, the armada assembled—4,126 assault and landing craft, 736 auxiliary vessels, 864 merchant ships—and a million fighting men were standing by. D-Day was to be 5th June. Then, inevitably, the weather took a hand; low cloud and squalls of rain swept across the Channel, and Overlord was postponed. For twenty-four hours, in the Solent, at Spithead, Portland, Torbay and other English ports, the invasion forces waited.

Some of the vessels in the mighty fleet which set course for Normandy on 6th June had helped to take the soldiers off the beaches of Dunkirk four long years before, and for them it was a triumphal return. Since those days of withdrawal and defeat, ships flying the Red Duster had been engaged in three great Allied amphibious operations—against North Africa, Sicily and Salerno—and Overlord was the greatest of them all, perhaps the greatest in military history. Miraculously, their losses of barely one per cent were fewer than in any of those earlier invasions.

Coasters, whose customary employment lay in carrying coal or potatoes between Liverpool and Ireland, had their masts and derricks strengthened, to enable them to load and carry thousands of field guns, white-starred armoured vehicles and trucks for the troops in Normandy. The Allied Air Forces commanded the skies above the assault route, the beaches, and deep into France. The Luftwaffe's impact was minimal, and the few U-boats, E-boats

and midget submarines which set out from their Bay of Biscay bases, with orders to attack the invasion fleet, were harried by aircraft all the way. Theirs was a hopeless, if not a suicidal, mission.

To put the Allied armies ashore, to breach the walls of Hitler's Fortress Europe, was an historic feat of arms, and Operation Overlord did not end on D-Day. From 6th June onwards, a constant shuttle service of supply and reinforcement had to be maintained. The 12,000 ton *Llangibby Castle*, a Landing Ship (Infantry) Large, which had carried 1,590 Canadian and British soldiers to Juno Beach on D-Day, made fifty Channel crossings in the next six months, carrying over 100,000 troops. The Union Castle mail ship, built in 1929, was a real Red Ensign veteran: she had been requisitioned by the Ministry of Transport in 1940, and employed as a transport between the UK and Africa, and later Canada, for her first two years in service. In January 1942, with over 1,400 troops aboard, she had been torpedoed in the North Atlantic, and both her stern and her rudder blown away; she had been steered by her diesel engines for 3,400 miles, at a steady nine knots, first to the Azores and eventually Gibraltar, where, after some repairs aft but still without a rudder, she had joined a slow convoy for the Clyde. The seamanship of her Captain, R.F. Bayer, on that voyage had brought him the award of the CBE. Ten months later, converted to the role of "assault transport", and carrying eighteen LCAs on her decks, the "Gibby" had sailed with the first fast convoy to North Africa on Operation Torch. After the troops had been put ashore, as the cook/steward Jack Armstrong remembers: "We were used for target practice by an enemy gun battery on one of the mountains for an hour or so. The shells landed all around us, but they only scored a hit on the after end of the boat deck; sadly, that hit killed our electrician. Our guns fired back, but they didn't have the range. We laid a smoke-screen and got away in that."

A few days after Overlord, one merchant master, whose coaster had just completed her fourth Channel crossing with a load of petrol cans, replied when he was asked how the war was going for him: "I won't be sorry to get back to coal."

In his Christmas broadcast of 1944 to the British people, King George VI, bravely overcoming his tendency to stammer, spoke these words: "Never was I more proud of the title 'Master of the Merchant Navy and Fishing Fleets' than at the time of the Normandy landings, when thousands of merchant seamen, in hundreds of ships, took across the Channel on that great adventure, our armies and their equipment."

The merchant seamen's part in the European war should have ended with VE-Day. It would have done so but for the action of Kapitänleutnant Emil Klusmeier, commanding a new Type XXIII U-boat, who, late in the evening of 7th May, found one last convoy sailing out of Edinburgh into the Pentland Firth, with all aboard rejoicing. Klusmeier fired his torpedoes into the Canadian steamer *Avondale Park* and the veteran Norwegian tramp *Sneland I*, and twenty-three men died when they went down. Klusmeier was strictly out of order—Dönitz had ordered all U-boats to cease fire and surrender—and thus the Unterseebootewaffe ended the war the way it had begun, with the destruction of a defenceless ship.

On 4th April 1945, President Roosevelt reminded the American people that, on 22nd May 1819, the SS *Savannah* had sailed on the first Atlantic crossing under steam. It was also the date, in 1943, that Grossadmiral Dönitz gave the order withdrawing active U-boats from the Atlantic. That date, Roosevelt proclaimed, would thereafter be known and celebrated as National Maritime Day in honour of the wartime courage of the mercantile marine and the skill of those who built their ships. The proclamation was reinforced by President Clinton in 1994, when he urged Americans "to observe this day with appropriate programs, ceremonies, and activities and by displaying the flag of the United States at their homes and other suitable places." The President went on to request "that all ships sailing under the American flag dress ship on that day."

The British commemorated the Battle of the Atlantic on 22nd May 1993 in Liverpool and there are annual parades at the Merchant Navy Memorial at Tower Hill, London, in September and November. A 'Convoy of Trees' is being planted in Britain's National Memorial Arboretum, with a tree for each merchant ship lost.

Note: In this chapter, and elsewhere in this book, the term "gross tonnage" or "gross registered tonnage" is occasionally used. This means the entire internal capacity of a ship in tons of 100 cubic feet each. "Net tonnage" is the ship's gross tonnage less the cubic capacity of the internal space not available for cargo, such as the areas dedicated to the machinery, the crew and any passengers. "Deadweight" is the ship's carrying capacity in tons, and is usually about 50% greater than the gross tonnage. The tonnage of a warship is usually given as the "displacement", which means the vessel's total weight, as measured in accordance with the Archimedes principle.

The man in the wilderness asked me, / How many strawberries grow in the sea? I answered him, as I thought good, / As many as red herrings grow in the wood.
—nursery rhyme

There is a tide in the affairs of men, / Which, taken at the flood, leads on to fortune; / Omitted, all the voyage of their life / Is bound in shallows and in miseries.
On such a full sea we are now afloat, / And we must take the current when it serves. / Or lose our ventures.
—from *Julius Caesar* by William Shakespeare

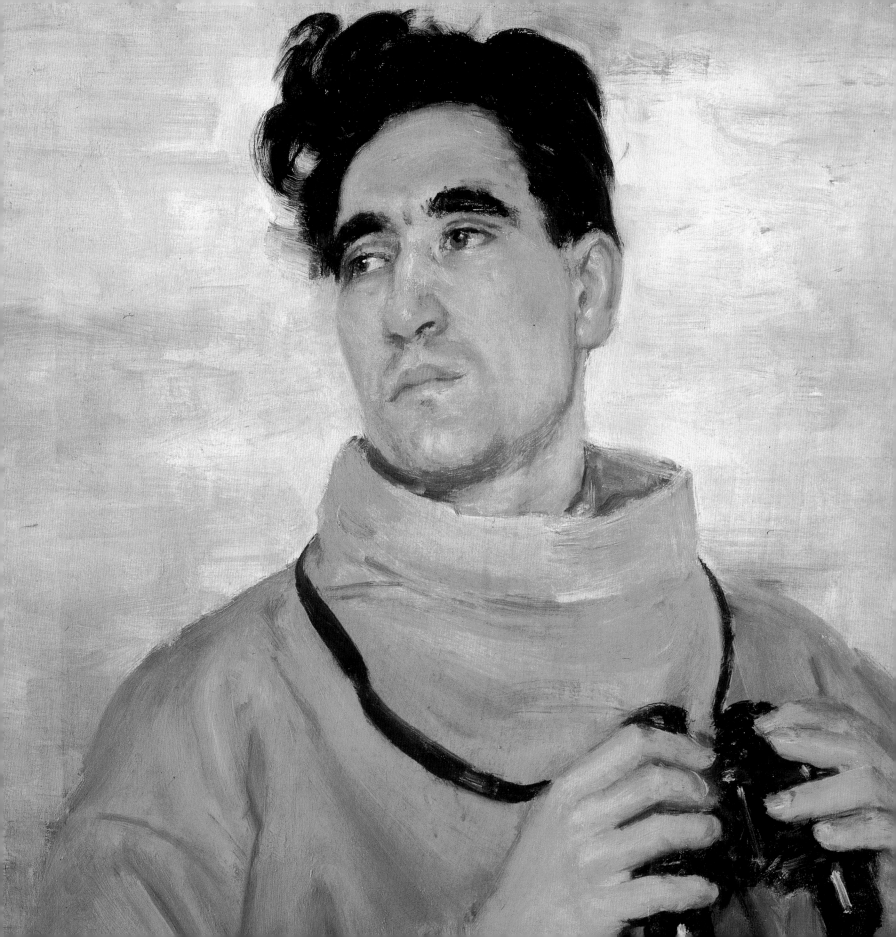

IN SEPTEMBER 1938, the British Government, foreseeing a need to reinforce the Merchant Navy, put out a call for volunteers with experience of the sea. The response was good and, within the year, a substantial pool of some 13,000 had been formed, including navigation officers, engineers, deck hands, cooks and stewards, ranging in age from teenage deck boys and apprentices to pensioners. They were soon needed, for when war was declared, 12,000 officers and men of the existing Merchant Navy promptly applied to join the fighting service. Many of them were members of the Royal Naval Reserve, which, according to one wardroom wit, was composed of people who were seamen but not gentlemen (the Royal Navy Volunteer Reserve, on the other hand, was said to consist of gentlemen who were not seamen), and the Merchant Navy version was that the Royal Navy were 'neither trying to be both.' The pool system, however, had its disadvantages: in the course of their service, the sailors might serve with a dozen different shipping lines, depending on whichever owned the ship they joined. Consequently, they lacked the feeling of belonging to a team, unlike their brothers in the Royal Navy, who had centuries of tradition, of battles fought and won, to stiffen their morale and their resolve.

When Jack Armstrong of Hull first went to sea in 1940, the Merchant Navy Pool had yet to be formed. "Seamen then," he said, "weren't allocated to a ship, and would sign on with any ship they could. Signing on was for a minimum of six months and a maximum of twelve, except for service overseas, which was for three years. But the contracts were one-way only, and owners could sign you off at any time, and in any British port. Once you signed on, you got an allotment note as an advance of pay, but since no-one had a bank account, you relied on traders and pubs to cash the allotment notes, usually at a cost of ten per cent. Paid leave wasn't introduced until 1943, and until then a seaman was paid off with his wages, minus any stoppages, plus his train fare home. Most men bought their rail tickets, and got drunk with what was left. In those days articles were signed at the Shipping Federation, which was always next to the Seamen's Home, and men hung around these buildings, waiting for a ship and listening to the grapevine. It was one of the ironic consequences of war that, when the Ministry of War Transport and the Pool came in, conditions, food and rates of pay immediately improved, and berths were allocated by the Pool."

At that time, the leave allowance was normally granted at the rate of two days for every month at sea, but it was always liable to be cut short by a telegram peremptorily ordering 'Report to Pool immediately'.

On board a merchant ship, the Captain (or Master) had command; his deck officers were normally the Chief Officer (or First Mate), the Second Officer (or Mate), responsible for navigation, and the Third Officer (or Mate), responsible for signals. They shared the bridge watches: the Chief Officer took the watch from 4 to 8 a.m., the Second from 12 to 4, and the Third from 8 to 12. The Radio Officer was responsible for WT communications. There would also probably be an Apprentice—a deck officer under training. The Boatswain was the senior deck rating, and under him were the Able (certified) and Ordinary (non-certified) Seamen and the deck boys. The Ship's Carpenter maintained the woodwork and plumbing above decks.

The Chief Engineer answered for the operation of the engines and ancillary equipment, the Second Engineer for their maintenance, and the Third for the electrics. These, with a Fourth Engineer, shared the engine room watches in the same way as the deck officers shared those on the bridge, and under their supervision came the Donkeyman (the senior engine room rating), the firemen, the trimmers (or stokers) and the greasers.

The Chief Steward was in charge of all catering,

# MERCHANT SAILORS

Land was created to provide a place for steamers to visit.
—from *Once Around The Sun* by Brooks Atkinson

For all that has been said of the love that certain natures (on shore) have professed to feel for it, for all the celebrations it has been the object of in prose and song, the sea has never been friendly to man. At most it has been the accomplice of human restlessness.
—from *The Mirror of the Sea* by Joseph Conrad

Canadian seamen received 25 cents a day 'hard laying' pay for corvette duty at sea.

I've had more fun at funerals than I did at sea.
—Reverend J.W.S.Wilson

left: *W.M.Ladbrooke, Able Seaman, Merchant Navy*, by Bernard B. Hailstone

right: The badge of the Merchant Navy, below: The Green Lantern restaurant and soda fountain, a popular spot with members of all the services in Halifax during the war.

left and below: The Allied Merchant Seaman's Club, Hollis Street, Halifax.

More than 30,000 Allied merchant seamen and naval personnel died in the Battle of the Atlantic.

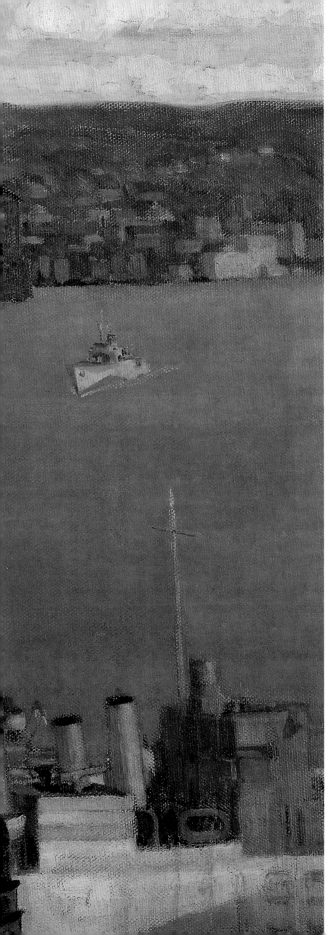

with a chief cook in charge of the galley, a second cook, and an assistant steward who served the officers and attended to their cabins.

At a quarter to eight in the evening of 3rd September 1939, the Donaldson Atlantic liner *Athenia* was 250 miles west of Inishtrahull, Ireland when she was torpedoed, without warning, by the German U-boat *U30*. The 13,000 ton liner, carrying 1,418 men, women and children, including 316 American citizens, was making 10 knots on a zig-zag course for Canada, where she was to be refitted as an armed merchant cruiser. The *Athenia* remained afloat until the early hours of the next morning, by which time a Norwegian freighter, two British destroyers, an American steamer and a motor yacht had arrived to rescue the survivors. Eighty-three civilian passengers, including twenty-two of the Americans, were lost. The eighteen members of the crew who also died were, like the passengers, unarmed civilians, and they were the first Merchant Navy casualties of World War II.

Those early deaths were to be multiplied a thousandfold and more within the next five years, nearly double those sustained in World War I. By the time VE-Day came in 1945, 22,490 British merchant seamen had been killed, plus 6,093 Indian Lascars and 2,023 Chinese; to these must be added 5,662 seamen from the USA, 4,795 from Norway, approximately 2,000 from Greece, 1,914 from the Netherlands, 1,886 from Denmark, 1,437 from Canada, 893 from Belgium, 182 from South Africa, 109 from Australia and 72 from New Zealand. The figures do not include the deaths of nearly 4,000 gunners of the Royal Navy and the Royal Artillery who lost their lives while serving on board merchant ships, nor the many thousands incurred by neutral countries.

Seamen sailing under the Red Ensign of the Merchant Navy came from every part of the British Isles, but mainly from the coastal conurbations,

As we honor the heroes of D-Day and World War II, it is fitting to include among them the civilian American merchant mariners who sailed in harm's way to supply the needs of our Allied fighting forces...Their sacrifices were crucial to victory, as were the unparalleled efforts of American shipbuilding. —President William J. Clinton, 19th May 1994

More than 78 million long tons of cargo left United States ports in 1944. About 50 per cent was for the Army, 10 per cent for the Navy, 30 per cent for lend-lease goods and the remainder was essential civilian cargo.

left: *Crane, Halifax harbour,* by Harold Beament.

24

the Clyde, Teesside and Tynemouth, Hull and Whitby, from Bristol and South Wales. They were joined by many Lascars from India and Africa, by Chinese and Arabs, by Africans, and by more than 50,000 who came from neutral or nominally allied countries. A memorial to their dead in two world wars stands on Tower Hill in London, close by the north bank of the Thames. Fittingly, the model for the statue on that monument was a man from Lewis, the Outer Hebridean island which gave so many of its sons to serve in Britain's navies and to die in Britain's cause.

At sea, their living conditions and accomodation were restricted and austere. In the tramp steamers, only the master and the chief engineer had their own cabins, with a toilet and a bath; the deck officers shared cabins amidships below the bridge, while the engineer officers' were above the engine room. The rest of the crew slept in two-tier iron-framed bunks below the forecastle head—not the most stable portion of the ship—usually with the firemen and greasers on the port side, and the seamen, the bosun and the carpenter to starboard, and they all queued up to use the head. Not for them the comforts enjoyed by the crew of the good ship *Mantelpiece*, as described by W.S. Gilbert in *The Bab Ballads*:

A feather bed had every man,
Warm slippers and hot water can,
Brown Windsor from the captain's store,
A valet, too, for every four.

"It was the long Atlantic trips that were worst for cabin conditions," said one seaman, "especially on the lower decks, where the portholes couldn't be opened. As many as eight men ate, slept, smoked and broke wind, and generally lived in those 'glory holes' with their damp clothes. The air was thick and foul, like in a submarine. It was heaven to stand up on deck and breathe in the fresh air. There was no real recreation, only an occasional game of cards—cribbage was the favourite—just

four hours on watch, eight hours off, with extra work like chipping, cleaning and painting in off-duty hours. Any spare time was spent on private chores and sleep."

The navigation equipment on a tramp was usually the minimum required: a sextant, a compass, a sounding lead and a chronometer. No radio direction-finding sets, and certainly no radar, and yet, with the basic kit they had, the tramps' 2nd Officers (usually responsible for the navigation) somehow found their way across the oceans of the world.

The merchant seaman's life was one which, in spite of its hardships and its dangers, always held a suggestion of adventure and romance. It did not matter that he would never be a rich man: he

The sea is a great maker of men: men of courage and of grit, men of authority and resource, men of nerve, strength and muscle fitness. For fools she has no use; nor for slackers, nor yet the timid. These she either breaks or casts aside.
—Joseph Conrad

below and left:
Entertainment for service personnel in wartime Halifax

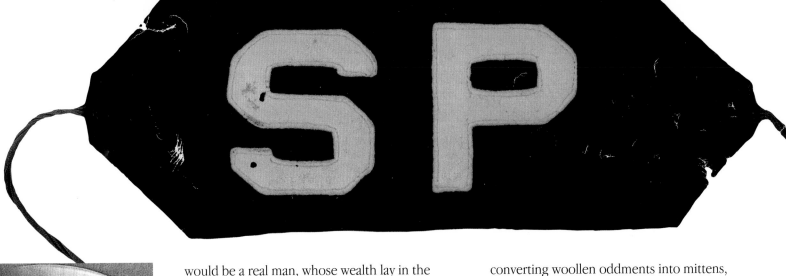

The sea never changes and its works, for all the talk of men, are wrapped in mystery.
— from *Typhoon* by Joseph Conrad

would be a real man, whose wealth lay in the depth of his experience, the breadth of his environment, the good opinion of his shipmates. He was a man, often like his father and grandfather before him (for the call of the sea tends to echo down the years in certain families), who would roam the oceans of the world, who would know the exotic fascinations of many distant places—a man who would always have a new horizon.

He might suffer badly, sometimes fatally, from extremes of temperature—heat exhaustion in the engine room, hypothermia on deck—and from the sort of injuries that were liable to afflict men who habitually handled machinery on tossing, rolling surfaces. Then, he would be dependent on such knowledge of doctoring as the master had acquired in his years at sea, or could assimilate from reading the Board of Trade's "Medical Guide for Captains". But if he should be so careless or unfortunate, in his time ashore, to contract a venereal disease (euphemistically described as lady sickness), it would be considered a "self-inflicted injury", and the man would be strictly on his own.

The stalwart efforts of the Merchant Navy seamen, and of their colleagues in the fishing fleet, did not go unrecognised within their own communities— in Britain alone, at least 150 charities were dedicated to their welfare, and thousands of women devoted their spare time to converting woollen oddments into mittens, scarves and Balaclava helmets for the sailors' comfort. Such organisations as the British Sailors Society and the American British War Relief Society did rather better with a supply of woollen jumpers, socks and gloves, undergarments, oilskins, shoes and caps. In the major ports throughout the Empire and Commonwealth where merchant shipping docked, in all the Allied and in many neutral countries, clubs and canteens were opened to cater for the seamen's brief periods ashore. Nor did service in the Merchant Navy go entirely unrewarded by the British Crown. Between them, the officers and men won 5 George Crosses, 18 Distinguished Service Orders, 213 Distinguished Service Crosses, 1,077 Orders of the British Empire, 1,211 MBEs, 1,717 British Empire Medals, 50 CBEs, and 10 Knighthoods.

No such honours came the way of Jack Armstrong, the mess steward from Hull, but he did once come within hailing distance of the epitome of British glory, Winston Spencer Churchill. "In August 1941," said Jack, "we were en route for the UK from Halifax, when there were emergency warnings that an enemy warship was approaching, and the convoy was to scatter. It takes a while to alter course at low speed, then to accelerate, and by the time this warship arrived, the convoy was a shambles. The warship turned out to be the *Prince of Wales*, with Churchill on board, sailing home from a secret meeting with President Roosevelt.

Mr. Churchill may have wondered why he didn't get a rousing welcome when his ship and her escorts passed through the convoy and why it was in such a shambles. In fact, our remarks were uncomplimentary, because of the panic he had caused. I suppose the *Prince of Wales* was maintaining radio silence so as not to reveal his presence, but we all thought he should have kept away from us."

For each year of the war, a Merchant Navy master spent an average of 125 days at sea. The Atlantic Battle was fought over 4,000,000 square miles of ocean.

In 1942, the British Merchant Navy had a strength of 120,000 officers and men—the equivalent of eight Army divisions. In common with his American equivalent, the British merchant sailor had the right to decline the first two ships offered to him, but must take the third if he wanted to

left: The US Navy Shore Patrol kept a watch on off-duty naval personnel, below: Eye-catching cast members of the Marcus variety show in Halifax.

Eternal Father, strong to save, / Whose arm hath bound the restless wave, Who bidd'st the mighty ocean deep / Its own appointed limits keep; / O hear us when we cry to thee For those in peril on the sea.
—W. Whiting

remain in the pool (or on the union register), and, while he so remained, he was exempt from service in the armed forces. An Able Seaman's pay was £12 a month, less than half that of his American counterpart, and slightly more than half that received by a Sergeant Pilot in the RAF. The life of an American merchant seaman was insured by his Government for $5,000, and his disablement for

$2,000 more; any insurance carried by a British merchant seaman, he paid for himself. And while the British Merchant Navy refused to recognise that overtime existed, let alone reward it, the American Merchant Marine paid it a rate of 85 cents for every hour worked over 44 a week, and added war bonus payments of 100% for service in the North Atlantic and the Mediterranean, 80% for

the Pacific and the Indian Ocean, and 40% in other theatres. The British seaman had to be content with an overall War Risk Bonus of £10 per month.

A Chief Officer's monthly salary was seldom more than £30. Until equity prevailed almost half-way through the war, when a seaman's ship went down, he at once came off the pay-roll. Some senior officers stayed on it if they were employed by the shipping companies. The majority, however, were employed by the Pool and suffered in the same way as the crews. A seaman's living space afloat was similar to that of a soldier or an airman in a German prisoner-of-war camp. Indeed, the near three thousand who were captured found no great difference when they were incarcerated in the German Navy's

left and below: Merchant seamen of the motor vessel *Empire Unity,* splicing wire and doing their washing.

The Shell tanker *Corbis* returned from Aruba in August 1941 and docked at Grangemouth refinery to unload. I went ashore to have a tooth extracted, and when I got back the ship had gone. I had to take the train to Inverness, on to Edinburgh, spending the night in both, then to Achnasheen to catch a bus to Loch Ewe, where the *Corbis* was waiting for another convoy to assemble. It cost me a week's pay.
—Jack Armstrong, tanker steward, Merchant Navy

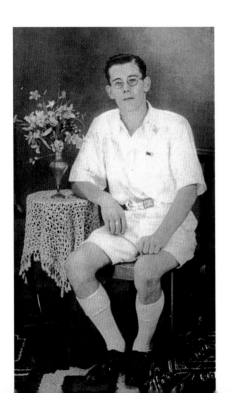

below: Steward Jack Armstrong, in 1945, right: One of his MN Account of Wages statements.

camps, Milag und Marlag near Sandbostel, apart from missing the motion of the sea.

In a typical Atlantic convoy, the vessels would move in columns, between nine and twelve in number, like an army on the march. The columns would be separated by 1,000 yards, with the ships 600 yards apart, so the convoy might present a frontage of four-and-a-half miles and be one-and-a-half miles deep. "Don't straggle, gentlemen," the ship-masters would be told before departure at the Convoy commodore's conference, "and don't romp ahead. Don't make smoke—remember, one careless stoker can get us all in trouble." And, once at sea, the master of a ship which strayed out of dressing or alignment without good reason could expect a verbal broadside, either from the Commodore or the commander of the escort.

For a wartime airman, the worst fear, short of death or maiming, was of drifting down on a parachute into a hostile country a long way from home; for a merchant sailor, it was the thought of being alone on the ocean, floating in a life raft, far out of sight of any land. It was this predicament in which the only survivor of the tramp *Baron Blythswood* found himself on 21st September 1940.

The Unterseebootwaffe's "happy time" was at its height when the 41-ship convoy HX72, in the Western Approaches bound for Britain, sailed into the sights of Kapitänleutnant Günther Prien, in command of *U47*. Prien called in the wolfpack, which included Kovettenkapitän Otto Kretschmer's *U99*, and the slaughter began. In the next seven hours, twelve ships went down, and the *Baron Blythswood* was one of Kretschmer's kills. Loaded with iron ore, she sank within a minute. Later, in the daylight, one of Kretschmer's deck-watch called him to the bridge. "A tiny raft," Kretschmer recorded in his Kriegstagebuch or war diary, "was wallowing in the swell with an oar erected as a mast, from which a white shirt was flying in the wind. Holding onto the makeshift

mast to keep his balance, was a lone man in his underwear."

It was that lone man's lucky day. Kretschmer's crew took him aboard *U99*, wrapped him in blankets, and put him to bed with a large glass of brandy for company. When he awoke, they clothed him, supplied him with food and water, and put him aboard a lifeboat from the tanker *Invershannon*, which had been Kretschmer's first victim in the convoy. With a shout of "Good luck" and a course to steer for Ireland, Otto Kretschmer, sped away.

There are other stories in the Merchant Navy annals of solitary survivors, one of which described the adventures of an able seaman, whose ship was sunk in the Spring of 1943 and who found himself alone in the Atlantic with a substantial piece of wreckage, one whole cabbage and a snapshot of his wife. Occasionally munching a leaf of the cabbage, drinking rain water and melted hail or snow, and talking to the photo, he survived until a ship came by eighteen days later. Another story, even more remarkable, was of a Chinese steward, whose ship, the *Benlomond*, sailing west from Cape Town, was torpedoed on 23rd November 1942. The steward subsisted for no less than 133 days on the small provisions which he found on his raft, augmented by whatever fish and seagulls he could catch. He was rescued by a Brazilian fisherman, and taken to hospital in Belem, just south of the equator, and lived to tell the tale. Some ten months later, that sturdy man's record was exceeded, although only by a day, by two survivors of the *Fort Longueuil*, sunk by *U532* in the Indian Ocean. Their raft drifted ashore on the island of Sumatra, where their epic journey sadly ended in being captured and imprisoned by the Japanese.

It was once slanderously said of the Merchant Navy that its ships were "manned by the pickings of the prisons and officered by the sweepings of the public schools", in which case Britain had

left: The Halifax Knights of Columbus all-services centre in wartime, below: Lookout descending from the crow's nest of a merchant vessel.

# HUNTERS

As long as I can remember, I wanted to go to sea, and dreamed, when I saw large merchant ships pass my home town in Holland, that some day I would be on the bridge of one of them. But my father, who fished for a living his whole life, was not in favour of this. My grandfather and my uncles all had lost their lives while fishing in the North Sea. My grandfather was steamed over by an English ship in heavy fog while fishing in November 1929. Then, when I was seven I got an eye infection, which put me in a Rotterdam hospital for several weeks. When a doctor there asked me what I wanted to become, and I told him I wanted to be a ships' officer, he told me that I would have to find another profession.
—Peter Wakker, engineer

right: *Clear The Deck* by Stephen Bone, far right: The wings of the U.S. Civil Air Patrol which helped hunt U-boats off the American east coast during WWII.

BOTH GROSSADMIRAL Erich Raeder, Commander-in-Chief of the Kriegsmarine, and Admiral Karl Dönitz, Commander of the Unterseebootwaffe, would have been better pleased if the Führer's invasion of Poland in September 1939 had been deferred for several years. Raeder wanted time for the building of a battle fleet which would match the Royal Navy in numbers, as it already did in equipment. Dönitz, on the other hand, was convinced that the way to beat the British was with submarines not battleships. However, he had first to persuade Raeder and, through him, Adolf Hitler, and then he needed time to build up his U-boat fleet. Unfortunately for Dönitz, Hitler's policy towards Poland, as one of his senior staff later revealed, "was governed by impatience and rage". The Führer had the bit between his teeth, and there was no stopping him.

As a result, when the war began, the Royal Navy outnumbered the Kriegsmarine by 7 to 1 in battleships (the great new *Bismarck* and *Tirpitz* had yet to be completed), 6 to 1 in cruisers and 9 to 1 in destroyers. Dönitz's U-boat fleet totalled fifty-six (one fewer than the Royal Navy's submarine arm), and less than half of those were capable of operating beyond the Baltic and European coastal waters. However, production steadily increased, and, by the first few months of 1941, U-boats were emerging from the shipyards at the rate of ten a month. Furthermore, with the acquisition of the ports on the western coast of France in the early summer of 1940, they were no longer confined to operations within range of their bases on the North Sea and the Baltic coasts, and could patrol for days far out in mid-Atlantic. Dönitz had long dreamed of a fleet of 300 long-range U-boats—a third of which, as he envisioned them, would be on station, a third en route going out or coming back, and a third being re-equipped at base. It was a dream that nearly came true in the Spring of 1942, and it was as well for the Allies that it did not.

When Germany signed the London Submarine Agreement in 1935, she had undertaken to observe the terms of the Geneva Convention in regard to submarine warfare. This meant that a U-boat commander was obliged to stop a target merchant vessel before he attacked it, to order the crew to their lifeboats and, when he had sunk the vessel, by whatever means, to ensure that the lifeboats would hold all the survivors. Such scrupulous conduct, although initially followed by some of the early U-boat commanders (but certainly not all), did not last long in the escalating violence of the war at sea.

From the middle of June 1940 until October of that year, the crews of the U-boats enjoyed what was always thought of later as their "happy time". In those months, they wrought havoc on the oceans of the world, and sank over 300 Allied vessels with a GRT (gross registered tonnage) of 1,457,861. It seemed then that the British had no answer to Die Rudeltaktik—the *modus operandi* of the wolfpacks—for which Dönitz, himself a U-boat commander in 1918, had schemed and planned throughout the 1930s. Six or seven U-boats would form a "stripe" across what was judged at Dönitz's headquarters in Lorient, to be a convoy's likely course, based on air reconnaissance or radio intercepts by Beobachtundienst (B-dienst). Once a U-boat commander had sighted the convoy, he would advise the other U-boats by radio. The pack would shadow it, keeping their distance, until the time came to attack—usually at night and from the darker side of the horizon.

While the British had developed the convoy system, and used it successfully for six centuries or more, it seems clear, with hindsight, that in 1940 the Royal Navy did not fully appreciate the deadly threat of the wolfpacks. Ship-to-ship communications were totally inadequate, and the merchant masters—a sturdily independent breed of men—occasionally turned a blind eye to their orders and made their own decisions. In the early

Even in peacetime an average of 1,100 ocean-going ships are lost each year. But in wartime Great Britain alone lost three ships a day during 1917, and 2,479 British merchant vessels went down during the first World War. During April, 1917, the number of Allied and neutral ships which were sunk totaled 430. The first two weeks of World War II saw 27 British merchant ships go under. In 1917 sixteen British merchant ships were sunk in a single day.
—from *HOW TO ABANDON SHIP* by Phil Richards and John J. Banigan

all: Aboard German U-boats on patrol during the Battle of the Atlantic.

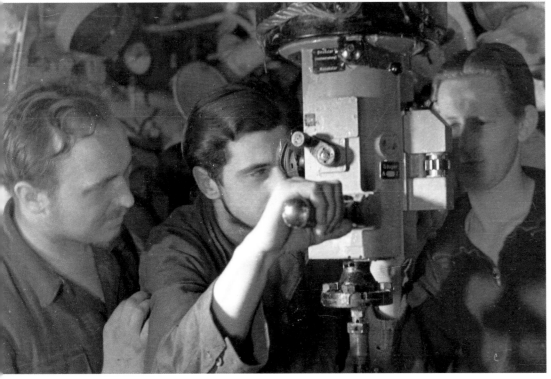

days, air support was almost non-existent. The only escort ships available were the little Flower Class corvettes and a number of passenger liners which had been converted, by the mounting of a few guns, into AMCs (Armed Merchant Cruisers—or 'Admiralty Made Coffins', as the seamen called them). Such a vessel was the 16,000 ton *Rawalpindi*, once of the P. & O. line, which was sunk on 23rd November 1939 after a heroic fight with the German battlecruisers *Scharnhorst* and *Gneisenau*, between Iceland and the Faroes in the North Atlantic. The *Rawalpindi* was the first of fifteen AMCs to be sunk in the opening eighteen months of war.

Because U-boats were still thought of as essentially operating under water, too much faith was placed in the combination of the Asdic underwater sensor (later known as sonar) and depth-charges as the main defence against them. While they were attacked by gunfire, neither Asdic nor depth-charges were of any use against a U-boat operating on the surface after dark.

It was only after the grim days and nights of the 1940s that the organisation of the convoys and of their protection began to meet the German threat. Serviceable ship-to-ship radio telephony then became available, with search radar devices, high frequency direction-finding apparatus HF/DF (known as "Huff-duff") for intercepting radio traffic between U-boats, well-equipped rescue ships with medicos on board sailing with each convoy, all-illuminating Leigh lights on aircraft, and "snowflake" flares fired by rockets and suspended on parachutes to light up the night for the escorts and the trained gunners on the merchant ships. Furthermore, the Royal Canadian Navy were providing valuable aid by taking over the Atlantic escort duties as far as 40 degrees west.

By the end of May 1941, the German battleship *Bismarck* was one hunter which would hunt no more. Her career had been brief and not

uneventful. On 24th May, she had sunk the mighty battlecruiser HMS *Hood* in the Denmark Strait with half-a-dozen salvoes of 15-inch shells, and with a dozen more she had driven off the battleship HMS *Prince of Wales*. She would have broken out into the wide Atlantic had she not been spotted by an American pilot, flying an RAF Catalina. The aircraft carrier HMS *Ark Royal*'s gallant airmen in their elderly Fairey Swordfish bi-planes slowed her down with their torpedoes, and on 27th May she was sunk by gunfire from the battleships HMS *King George V* and HMS *Rodney*. The event held far more significance in the war at sea than the sinking of one battleship, for its effect was to disillusion Hitler with Raeder's surface fleet, and to make him look with favour on Dönitz's U-boats.

In December 1941, at Pier Head in Liverpool, the survivors of the *Bismarck* (only about a twentieth of her complement of over 2,000) were taken

aboard the merchantman *Moreton Bay* of the Aberdeen and Commonwealth line. Her holds, fitted with iron bars, were to serve as cells when she took the German sailors to Canada as prisoners of war. "We had always hoped," said steward Jack Armstrong, "that we wouldn't meet the *Bismarck*, and yet when the seamen arrived, there was a comradeship between us. They made models out of anything to hand and exchanged them for whatever we could give. They even gave a Christmas concert for the crew. We knew they were the enemy, but to us they were seamen, and the sea has its own fraternity. Their military guards could not quite understand this."

It was as well for the Allies that the Unterseeboot-waffe had on-going trouble with the guidance and ignition systems of its torpedoes. For the first two years of war, until Dönitz at last got some action from the Kriegsmarine's torpedo development establishment, many of the torpedoes were either not detonating or were running at the wrong depth for a strike. It was not until mid-September 1943 that the U-boats were equipped with the acoustic Zaunkönig torpedo, designated "Gnat" (for German Naval Acoustic Torpedo) by the Allies, which, once launched, could home in on the sound of any motor. The British, however, produced a simple but effective counter-measure— a dinghy towed astern containing a noisy donkey engine, called a "Foxer", which fooled the Gnat's homer.

It was not until strong air support became available, and the American Hudsons, long-range Liberators and Catalinas joined the British Sunderlands and Ansons on ocean patrol, that the hunting U-boats were obliged to "go down into the cellar" more and more often, and to stay below the surface longer. Then, at last, the Asdic and depth-charges of the escort warships came into their own. By the end of the war, depth-charges dropped or thrown from ships had sunk 158

William Dawson, a company director in Sunderland, England, and Bill Wilson, a vicar in Yorkshire, were shipmates aboard the MV *Empire Lugard* bound from Trinidad for New York with a cargo of bauxite, when, at midnight on 13th September 1942, she was torpedoed by *U558* under the command of Günther Krech, and sank in just twelve minutes. Captain Krech sank 20 Allied vessels, with a total tonnage of 130,000, between 1941 and 1945. In July 1943, the *U558* was herself attacked and sunk in the Bay of Biscay by a Halifax bomber dropping depth charges. Of the sub's 46-man crew, only three survived, including the Krech. Of the *Empire Lugard* crew, all but two were rescued within two days. Forty years later, Dawson and Wilson were reunited and decided to form a survivor's club of fellow *U558* victims, the *U558 Association*. They contacted Krech in Wuppertal, Germany, and he offered to help with their research. Of Krech, Wilson commented: "It fascinates me that he coolly observed us and fired on us. He was doing his job, something he had been trained for. I remember our ship keeling over and we jumped for the lifeboat. I vaguely

remember feeling afraid but I cannot feel any anger towards that German."

At 1300 we were met by a minesweeper, sent to a predesignated point to guide us through the mine-infested waters to Lorient. Silently, we sailed and floated toward the large crowd lining the quay. Our comrades-in-arms stood by in gray-green uniforms, navy blues, and a variety of battle dress. Many girls—nurses from our military hospital—were waiting for us with flowers. How satisfying it was to be expected, how good it was to have survived!
—from *Iron Coffins* by Herbert A. Werner

all: WWII U-boat shelters in the Biscay ports of Saint Nazaire, Lorient and La Pallice, far left: *A U-Boat Lying in Drydock, St Nazaire, France, 1941* by Adolph Bock.

U-boats and, together with those launched from aircraft, had accounted for 42.8% of all U-boat sinkings. On many occasions, a U-boat was depth-charged for hour after hour, while the commander turned and twisted, trying to evade the next deadly salvo.

U575, for example, was hunted for eighteen hours, and eventually escaped, but on 29th February 1944, the long-serving U358 was sunk after a search that lasted for a whole day and a half.

Korvettenkapitän Werner Henke's U515 reportedly reached 250 metres (about 820 feet), and Herbert Werner claimed 280 metres in command of U230. The water pressure at 600 feet—the authorised safe diving depth—is about 200 tons on each square yard.

Excellent weapon platform though it was, a U-boat under water had a number of weak points: first, its speed was cut by half; second, it was blind, and dependent on the hydrophones for warning of approach by other vessels; third, when the boat went deep, its structural integrity was jeopardised by exhausts, inlets, glands and vents in the pressure hull. "Every noise was strange," said one U-boat commander, "and every creak seemed to herald the end." All the while, in the cramped crew compartments, the air became fouler and the temperature hotter. Eventually, starved of amperes for the batteries and oxygen for the crew, the commander had to blow tanks and face the music on the surface. Furthermore, a U-boat could not hover: it had to have motive power, diesel or electrical, for its hydroplanes and rudders to be effective.

Because more of them were built than any other type, the VIIC, long, sleek and sinister in aspect, was the main weapon in Admiral Dönitz's U-boat fleet. Its heart was the control room, housing the attack and navigation periscopes, and holding rows of levers, wheels and buttons for steering and balancing, surfacing and diving. A ladder gave access through a hatch to the conning tower

above. The engine rooms were aft—a pair of diesels, each developing 1,400 horse power, and two electric motors giving 750 horse power between them. Amidships were the galley, the radio and hydrophone shacks, the commander's compartment, and quarters for the 1st and 2nd Officers and the Chief Engineer; the bow compartment served as a workshop, as reserve

left: HMCS *Penetang* on convoy duty in the North Atlantic in 1944, below: A depth charge from a Canadian escort ship explodes during the Battle of the Atlantic.

torpedo stowage, and part accomodation for the forty-man crew—the deck hands, control room staff, "mixers" (the torpedo men), telegraphists and "stokers" (or engine room artificers). There were never enough bunks to house them all at once, so as each man came off watch he took over a "hot bunk" from the man who was relieving him.

Between eleven and fourteen torpedoes were carried, and life in the fore-ends became a little less cramped and uncomfortable after some of them had been fired and at least a man could almost stand upright. With the whole load of torpedoes, either gone or in their tubes, the men could even set up a table in the fore-ends.

left: *Catalina* by
Norman Wilkinson,
below: A U.S. Navy
PBY Catalina flying
boat on patrol in WWII.

This was the self-same Catalina, recovering from its honourable wounds, which had shadowed the *Bismarck* for twenty hours on May 24-25. Although ceaselessly attacked by the four aircraft from the *Bismarck* and riddled with anti-aircraft fire, it had remained on patrol for nearly a whole day until a Short Sunderland arrived as a great relief. Countless squadrons of our aircraft— the flying boats of the Coastal Command—have flown untold numbers of hours across the seas; but no flight was more memorable. No war flight had so thrilled the world. —from *Atlantic Battle* by Collie Knox

43

below: U.S. Navy PB4Y-1s on a Fort Worth, Texas assembly line, right: The cockpit of a Lockheed Hudson. Both types flew WWII convoy patrols.

The *Admiral Scheer* was a 10,000 ton German 'pocket battleship' with a draught of 23 feet, which enabled her to lie in shallow waters usually denied to warships with her sort of armament—six 11 inch, eight 5.9 inch and six 4.1 inch guns, eight torpedo tubes, plus two spotter aircraft. At a cruising speed of 15 knots, she had a range of 10,000 miles. She was designed to be a convoy raider, and her Captain, Theodor Krancke, knew that her task was to hit and run. When she emerged from the Baltic, and passed through the Denmark Strait into the Atlantic on 1st November 1940, her target was the convoy HX84, which had left Halifax on 28th October and was reported by

below: CAM *Empire Tide*'s Sea Hurricane, and the pilots, Flt. Lt. D.R.Turley-George, (left) and Fl. Off. C. Fenwick, right: A Catapult Aircraft Merchant ship.

B-dienst to be in the Western Approaches, sailing east-north-east for Britain at a steady nine knots. The thirty-seven ships of the convoy, which included eleven tankers, were arrayed in nine columns, with the Commodore, the retired Rear-Admiral H.B. Maltby, flying his flag in the *Cornish City* at the head of the centre column. The convoy's sole protection, once the Canadian destroyers had left them in mid-ocean, was the seven six-inch guns of the 14,000 ton armed merchant cruiser *Jervis Bay*, stationed between the fourth and fifth columns.

The *Jervis Bay*, built by Vickers Armstrong at Barrow in Furness and launched in January 1922,

below: A U.S. Navy K-Type blimp on anti-submarine patrol above an Allied North Atlantic convoy.

47

"The *Windsor Castle* (19,023 GRT) was off the Algerian coast on a trooping operation when she was attacked by a lone German bomber at about 2 am of 23rd March 1943. We'd had a Lockheed Hudson escorting us all day, and when the Ju-88 dropped its torpedo, it flew right across the convoy and not one shot was fired at it. I suppose everyone thought it was still the Hudson. I had come off watch at midnight, turned in below on 'A' deck and was very much asleep, wearing pyjamas because it was very warm and my cabin had no ports. There was a large muffled explosion, and the ship seemed to rock up and down, with an unusually quick motion. She always creaked below, but these were really loud creaks. The lights had failed, and it was bedlam outside. I grabbed my uniform jacket and a panic bag with Jerseys, long johns, et cetera and groped my way along the alley-way to the main stair-case and eventually out onto the boat-deck and up to the bridge.

There was a brilliant moon, with a moderate sea on the starboard beam. The tail end of the convoy and the escorts were passing by as we lost way. When I found the old man, Captain J.C. Brown, I said it was lucky we had a

was a handsome vessel, 549 feet long, with a breadth of 68 feet and a loaded draught of 33 feet. She had five oil-fired boilers, and her twin screws, driven by four turbines, gave her an operating speed of fifteen knots. She had been a favourite with passengers on the Aberdeen & Commonwealth line until the outbreak of war, when she had been one of the first cargo liners to be converted to the role of AMC. Now, her bright colours had been painted out, her brasswork dimmed and her stylish public rooms transformed. Although many of her officers and ratings were from her peacetime complement, she was under Royal Navy command, flying the White Ensign.

On 5th November 1940, it so happened that a banana boat, the *Mopan*, sailing from Jamaica with 70,000 bunches of the fruit so rarely seen in wartime Britain, was a few miles ahead of convoy HX84, and came within the range of Krancke's guns in the early afternoon. Two well-aimed shells persuaded the *Mopan*'s captain to abandon ship, but what made him refuse his Radio Officer's requests for permission to transmit a warning to HX84 remains in the realms of speculation. Unaware of the danger, the convoy was still making nine knots and steering 067 degrees when, shortly before 5 pm, the lookout on a merchantman sighted a warship approaching from the north. Within moments the *Scheer* was identified, and the Commodore ordered the convoy to scatter at full speed.

None knew better than Captain E.S. Fogarty Fegen, commanding the Jervis Bay, that the *Scheer* had far superior speed and firepower. He decided that the only hope was to try to keep the enemy engaged until dusk came to aid the merchant ships' escape. To commit his ship to such an action—inviting her destruction—was a hard decision, but Fegen did not hesitate. He was seen turning to port to steer directly at the enemy. *Sheer*'s first salvo destroyed the *Jervis Bay*'s

bridge, radio room and midships gun; it also blew off one of Fegen's legs and injured the other. He knew his ship was doomed, but he ordered the ship's surgeon to bind up his stump, and somehow made his way aft to direct the fire from the stern gun.

The battle continued for an hour and fifty minutes until the *Jervis Bay* rolled over and sank, still with her colours flying. Meanwhile, with darkness falling, thirty-two of the convoy's vessels had escaped. Fegen, with 33 of his officers and 156 members of his crew went down with the ship. 65 men were rescued by the Swedish freighter *Stureholm*, whose captain, Sven Olander, had seen a distress signal flashing from a raft and decided to turn back to the scene. The Victoria Cross was posthumously awarded to Captain Edward Stephen Fogarty Fegen.

When the *Stureholm* returned to Halifax with the *Jervis Bay*'s survivors, her master, all but one of her officers and fourteen of her crew refused to sail again. Next time she headed east out of Halifax, it was with her 2nd Officer in command and a crew made up from British survivors of HX84. She was torpedoed by *U96* in mid-Atlantic and there were no survivors.

For Captain Krancke, the HX84 sortie had not resulted in the devastating slaughter that was expected of him in Wilhelmshaven and Berlin. On Krancke's next patrol, beginning in December 1940, *Scheer*'s guns sank seventeen Allied ships in 160 days. It was the war's most successful sortie by a pocket battleship, and Krancke's reward was to be attached to Hitler's headquarters as Grossadmiral Raeder's representative. Meanwhile, in February 1941, the battle cruisers *Scharnhorst* and *Gneisenau* crept undetected through the Skagerrak into the North Atlantic and, in accordance with their Captains' orders, carefully avoiding any convoy escorted by a British warship, sank eleven merchantmen. In the same month, the heavy cruiser *Admiral Hipper* left her anchorage in Brest and set course for the Atlantic. 200 miles south-east of the Azores, she found the slow, unprotected nine-ship convoy SL64, homeward bound from Freetown, Sierra Leone. There were those on the merchant ships who identified the big ship approaching fast from the stern as the battle cruiser HMS *Renown*, which had been at anchor in Freetown when they left, come to give them escort, but they were quickly disillusioned when the German Naval Ensign was hoisted to *Hipper*'s masthead and she opened a devastating fire. By the time she moved away, and before a distress call could alert an avenging British warship, seven ships were sunk, two were badly damaged, and only one reached port.

And now the enemy hunters were becoming more numerous, and more widely spread. Six well-armed German surface raiders, *Pinguin* and *Atlantis*, *Komet* and *Orion*, *Kormoran* and *Thor*, disguised as neutral merchant ships, and serviced

below: Crew of the Fairey Swordfish, 'B' Baker, which sank a U-boat while flying from the escort carrier HMS *Chaser* in March, 1944.

warm night. He said 'Yes, Lester, thank the Lord that gave it to us.' He was a very religious man, who used to hold Bible classes in his cabin.

She began to settle by the stern, with all the way off her. The old man ordered 'abandon ship' and the alarm bells and the whistles sounded, with the feeling in the pit of the stomach that they always gave. I made my way to boat No. 2 on the port side, and she was lowered to the boat deck, filled with troops to capacity, and got clear after some difficulty with the forward falls. The ship's crew manned the oars and rowed to HMS *Loyal*, which had lowered her scrambling nets, so that all were soon on board.

The *Windsor Castle* didn't seem to be settling any more, and eventually fifteen of us went back aboard her with the old man, and waited until dawn, when the Chief Officer and I went down to inspect the engine room bulkheads. We walked through the cabin accommodation, doors wide open, with all the money, watches and personal things just left there. It was eerie. She had been hit in No. 5 hold, and the hatch covers had been blown sky-high. The main bulkhead was bulging with water spraying out from seams and rivets, and we didn't linger long. We

by supply ships lying close to neutral shores, roamed the seas. *Pinguin* was a menace in the Indian Ocean until 8th May 1941, when the heavy cruiser HMS *Cornwall* sent her down, sadly with some 200 Merchant Navy prisoners held below her decks. When *Thor* returned to Hamburg in April, her twelve kills in the South Atlantic had included HMS *Voltaire*, the last Armed Merchant Cruiser to be lost (the AMCs were withdrawn from fighting service soon after she went down and converted into troopships). *Komet* was guided by Soviet ice-breakers through the Kara Sea into the north-east passage, and together with the *Orion*, which returned to France from the Pacific in August after a record voyage of 127,000 miles in 570 days, she had sunk eighteen merchantmen. *Kormoran* in the South Atlantic, and *Atlantis* in the Indian Ocean, also had their successes, until both were sunk by warships in November 1941. With their destruction, the best days of the surface raiders were over.

*Thor*, however, made another patrol in the South Atlantic in February 1942 and, in a voyage of four months, sank a dozen ships. Her Captain, Günther Grumprich, despite Dönitz's edict, was always scrupulous in picking up survivors, and it was cruel luck for those he had aboard when, at the end of his patrol, he entered a Japanese port for servicing and refit: those ill-fated seamen were condemned to three long years in prison camps.

Dönitz was the master of U-boat tactics and deployment; he was also well served with target information, largely through the radio intercepts by B-dienst and to a lesser extent by air reconnaissance. What he lacked was intelligence material about Allied planning and intentions.

Although Dönitz oftened complained of inadequate support from the Luftwaffe,

spent a long morning expecting a few squadrons of Ju-88s to appear and finish her off, but nothing came. Nor did the tug from Algiers which was supposed to tow us in. About 2 pm, we were taken off, a tow rope was passed and made fast by a naval party, but as soon as the strain was taken up, the bulkhead gave and she started to settle by the stern again. The seamen jumped overboard and were picked up by the destroyer's sea-boat.

Back at Mers el Kebir, we were transferred to the *Rodney*, and I was put in the gun-room with the midshipmen, who weren't all that friendly (I was still wearing pyjama trousers with uniform jacket, so I can't entirely blame them), while we set course for Gibraltar. One last thought about the *Windsor Castle*: she was a beautiful ship, and I was very sad to see her go."

—John Lester, Deck Officer, Merchant Navy

left: *Attack on a Convoy, Seen from the Air 1941*, by Richard Eurich.

51

below: The Bangor Class minesweeper *Clayoquot* which was torpedoed and sunk just five miles from Halifax and five months before the war ended. Eight of her crew were lost. right: The *Windsor Castle* after being attacked by a German aircraft in March 1943.

Reichsmarschall Göring's aircrews had many successes in the war at sea. The Focke-Wulf Condors which prowled the North Atlantic and the Arctic, seeking out convoys and radioing their position to Lorient, and so to the wolfpacks, were a constant threat, and over waters nearer Germany, the torpedo bombers and the dive-bombers were notable for pressing home attacks.

In the Dr. Göbbels propaganda newsreels, the U-boat crews were always pictured dauntlessly putting out to sea, or returning triumphantly, with victory pennants flying from their masts. Their commanders were always saluting and waving, bearded faces smiling, as they stepped ashore from their patrols to be greeted by the Flotilla Commander and his staff (often by their Admiral), bouquets of flowers and a brass band playing.

After the fall of France the Germans gained access to all the harbours on the Atlantic and Bay of Biscay coasts, extending the range of the U-boats into the Atlantic by 500 miles. The British would have had a counter-measure if ports on the western coast of Ireland had been available, but the Dublin government insisted on preserving its position of neutrality. This despite the fact that the Irish were heavily dependent for money on the British treasury, as well as on British shipping for supplies, and that many Irishmen were serving with the British forces.

By VE-Day, 1,162 U-boats had been built in German shipyards, and 784 had been destroyed. Of 606 U-boats destroyed on the high seas US forces accounted for 132. 40,900 men had been recruited to serve in the Unterseebootewaffe, of whom 27,491 had been killed and another 5,000 made prisoners-of-war. The U-boat pens, with their twelve-foot thick walls and roofs of reinforced concrete, were the only places where German (and Italian) submarines could be truly safe in World War II.

We were visiting Liverpool for a minor refit and the crew was allowed shore leave. Jack Dusty and I went to Bootle by ferry to see a pen-friend at a WAAF balloon site. She had adopted our corvette, the *Sunflower*. We did not have the address of the balloon site, so we went to the headquarters of the balloons for that area. Being wartime, the corporal would not give us the address of the site we were looking for, so I asked to see the officer in charge (the corporal did not know we were not officers as we had our best uniforms on). I then told the officer that I was this WAAF's brother and had not seen her for three years. The officer at once told us the school where the WAAF was stationed, but said that we must leave immediately if an air raid happened. We had a very enjoyable afternoon with the WAAFs and ate their tea rations. Unfortunately, we missed the ferry back. We went to the local police to see if we could sleep in one of their cells, but they said we could not, so we ended up in an air raid shelter. Back on ship, we were put on report for being late returning. Our rum ration was stopped for seven days.
—C.H. Rayner, HMS *Sunflower*

## WILL SHE STARVE?

Since the declaration of war, many people have been laying in additional stocks of food, particularly sugar and tinned meats...So great has been the demand for sugar, in particular, that many shops have places a restriction on the amount that may be bought by any one customer.
—Falkirk *Herald*
9 September 1939

Dig! Dig! Dig! And your muscles will grow big, Keep on pushing the spade! Don't mind the worms, Just ignore their squirms, And when your back aches laugh with glee / And keep on diggin' / Till we give our foes a wiggin' / Dig! Dig! Dig! to victory.
—wartime song

right and far right: WWI poster art exhorting civilians to conserve food and aid the Allied war effort.

U.S. FOOD ADMINISTRATION

EAT MORE CORN, OATS AND RYE PRODUCTS— FISH AND POULTRY— FRUITS, VEGETABLES AND POTATOES BAKED, BOILED AND BROILED FOODS

EAT LESS WHEAT, MEAT, SUGAR AND FATS

TO SAVE FOR THE ARMY AND OUR ALLIES

THERE WERE TIMES from June 1940 onwards, and especially in the winter of 1942–43, when the German U-boat fleet came close to severing the North Atlantic lifeline, as it had so nearly done in 1917. The lessons learned then had not been lost upon the British government, and a scheme for food control was drawn up during the European crises of 1938 and 1939. Initially, it consisted of building up a reserve of foodstuffs, planning to control supply and distribution throughout the trade, and the creation of a Ministry of Food.

In July 1939, a series of Public Information Leaflets were issued to the public from the office of the Lord Privy Seal. Leaflet No. 4 was headed "Food in Wartime", which began: You know that our country is dependent to a very large extent on supplies of food from overseas. More than 20 million tons are brought into our ports from all parts of the world in the course of a year. Our defence plans must therefore provide for the protection of our trade routes by which those supplies reach us...

Another leaflet gave instructions about air raid warnings, the use of gas masks, lighting restrictions, fire precautions and evacuation of children from parts of London and some other towns. The last section dealt with food: It is very important that at the outset of an emergency people should not buy larger quantities of foodstuffs than they normally buy and normally require. The Government are making arrangements to ensure that there will be sufficient supplies of food, and that every person will be able to obtain regularly his or her fair share, and they will take steps to prevent any sudden rise in prices. But if some people try to buy abnormal quantities, before the full scheme of control is working, they will be taking food which should be available to others.

The scheme was implemented by the Ministry of Food as soon as World War II began, but not before there had been some panic buying, despite

We risk our lives to bring you food. It's up to you not to waste it.

J.P.Beadle

"A Message from our Seamen"

Potato Pete, Potato Pete, See him coming down the street, Shouting his good things to eat, 'Get your hot potatoes from Potato Pete.'

all exhortations. The plans embraced the issue through the Post Office of 45 million ration books, an import programme, transport arrangements, a trade licensing system and price controls. At local level, the scheme was to be administered by some 1,300 Food Control Committees and Food Offices in each Urban and Rural District. There were three types of ration book: for children under six, for all over six, and for certain workers who travelled round the country.

The first items to be rationed, on 8th January 1940, were butter and sugar (4 ounces per person per week of each), bacon and ham (12 ounces); meat went on the ration two months later, with children under six allowed eleven pennyworth per week, and others one shilling and sixpence worth; meat was soon followed by fats, cheese, tea, preserves, canned foods, cereals and biscuits, and the sugar ration was halved. Supplies of extra milk, cod liver oil and orange juice were reserved for young children, and expectant or nursing mothers.

In that October, at the time when autumn was turning to winter in the North Atlantic, sixty-three merchant ships went down, carrying over 352,000 tons of cargo, and every ship that sailed was under constant threat from the thousands of magnetic mines laid around the coasts of Britain, from attack by surface warships and aircraft, and, deadliest of all, from the silent menace of torpedoes launched from U-boats.

The War Cabinet's assessment of Britain's requirement for imports was 43,000,000 tons, and by October 1940, after the U-boat's "happy time", the tonnage reaching British ports had been reduced to 38,000,000. It was a serious shortfall, and potentially fatal to Britain's war effort.

In 1941, the Port of London was only functioning at a quarter of its full capacity, the Channel ports were under frequent air attack, while Bristol, Liverpool, Manchester and Clydeside were by no means immune. Winston Churchill was as gravely concerned in this arena of Britain's fight against the Nazis as in any other phase of the war. "Our losses," he reported to the War Cabinet, "are very heavy, and, vast as are our resources, the losses cannot continue indefinitely without seriously affecting our war effort and our means of subsistence." He minuted the First Lord of the Admiralty, Mr. A.V.Alexander: "I see that entrances of ships with cargo in January are less than half of what they were last January."

Rabbit Pie – 6ᵈ + 8ᵈ +Veg
Braised Liver 6ᵈ + 8ᵈ +Veg
Steak & Kidney Pie & Veg 6 & 8ᵈ
Sultana Roll – 2ᵈ
Rice Pudding 2ᵈ.
Lentil Soup 1ᵈ
Childrens Meals 4ᵈ

Churchill's selection of the vital data was perceptive, as it often was: once the losses of shipping exceeded the number of replacements, as indeed they had, the future for the British people was extremely grim. Early on, it had been decided that fresh fruit was out, while meat and eggs were in. But, to save cargo space and weight, imported meat had to be boned, eggs had to be shelled, and both commodities had to be dehydrated. This meant that meat from overseas would always look, and often taste, like sawdust, and that eggs could only be eaten scrambled or as omelettes. As for vitamin C, so essential to good health, green vegetables had to take the place of fruit, and every house dweller with the smallest piece of garden was encouraged, by official posters and through all the media, to give up his lawn and flower bed for the duration and "Dig for Victory". People with no gardens grew lettuces and radishes in their window boxes, and all manner of vegetables were cultivated on parkland, railway embankments, sports fields, and bomb sites. Meanwhile, the public were bombarded with "Food Facts" in the newspapers, "Kitchen Front" broadcasts on the radio and "Food Flashes" in the cinema.

The Ministry of Food employed artists to produce posters of "Doctor Carrot" and "Potato Pete", each jovially encouraging the consumption of his wares. While offering no great threat to Walt Disney as cartoon characters, they served to get the message across, especially to children, and their recipes for "carrot cookies" and "potato pie" were generally accepted, as were others from the Ministry for such dishes as "parsnip pudding", "cod pancakes", "marrow pudding", "potato piglets", "liver savoury", "eggless sponge" of which, predictably, the principal ingredients were "1 large raw potato, grated, and 2 medium raw carrots, grated".

It was a good day for the British, and for the cause of democracy, when, on 5th November

1940, Franklin D. Roosevelt was re-elected President of the United States. He had been Assistant Secretary of the Navy from 1913 to 1930, and, like Winston Churchill, who had been First Lord of the Admiralty at a crucial stage of World War I, he had an empathy with sailors, and an understanding of the sea. It was a bond between them of which the Englishman constantly reminded the American by signing all their

below: An English child putting kitchen waste into a salvage bin for pig food during WWII.

500 FOOD-EXTENDER WARTIME RECIPES

# 500
## FOOD-EXTENDER
# Wartime Recipes

**Food alternatives, Rationing hints, and Economical suggestions to help you serve nutritious, attractive wartime meals**

# ABC
## OF
# VICTORY GARDENS

BACKYARD FARMING
MADE EASY FOR ALL

OFFICIAL INFORMATION

AN AUTHORITATIVE
GUIDE TO HELP YOU
GROW VEGETABLES

# FOOD
# FOR VICTORY!

Examples of U.S. wartime cookery booklets and British food-related posters.

**DIG FOR VICTORY**

**BILE BEANS**

For Radiant HEALTH and a Lovely FIGURE

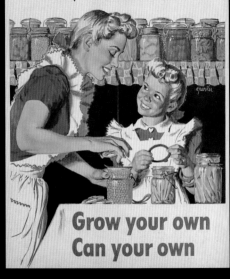

"We'll have lots to eat this winter, won't we Mother?"

**Grow your own Can your own**

THE *New* BOOK OF
REVISED RECIPES AND MENUS
Including A HANDY *Changeable*
TABLE OF POINT-VALUES FOR
*All* FOODS...

MEAT
in the meal
*for Health Defense*

Coupon
Cookery
by
Prudence
Penny

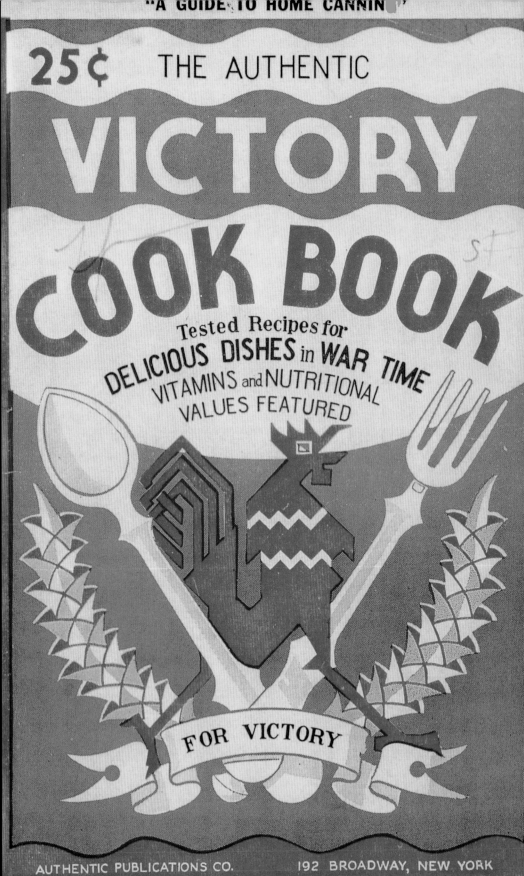

25¢   THE AUTHENTIC

VICTORY
COOK BOOK

Tested Recipes for
DELICIOUS DISHES in WAR TIME
VITAMINS and NUTRITIONAL
VALUES FEATURED

FOR VICTORY

AUTHENTIC PUBLICATIONS CO.   192 BROADWAY, NEW YORK

wartime correspondence as a "Former Naval Person".

Three days after the Japanese attack on Pearl Harbor, President Roosevelt announced: "In future, US air and naval forces will protect all shipping in their waters of whatever flag close to the US safety zone."

The passage of the "Lend-Lease" Bill through Congress, and its authorisation by Roosevelt on 11th March 1941, was acknowledged by Churchill with this heartfelt message: "Our blessings from the whole British Empire go out to you and the American nation for this very present help in time of trouble." Earlier, in September 1940, when one of Britain's major needs had been for Atlantic escort ships, a deal had been made between Washington and London which brought the Royal Navy the loan of fifty (later extended to 250) World War I American "four-stack" destroyers in return for a ninety-nine year lease to the USA of British bases in the Bahamas and the West Indies.

Meanwhile, in the summer of 1941, Churchill found it necessary to chide Lord Woolton, the Minister of Food, for reducing the meat ration; people, he protested, would be obliged to eat more bread, which would lead in turn to more cargo space being needed for imported wheat. "Let us also," he advised, "persuade the Americans to provide us with more pork." That was a year in which merchant shipping losses, including British, Allied and neutral vessels, amounted to 1,141 (over half of which were sunk by U-boats), with a gross tonnage of over four million.

The Women's Land Army, first formed in World War I, was reactivated, and thousands of "Land Girls", many in their teens, left their urban homes, their work in offices and factories, and went to work on farms throughout the country. Often, their accommodation was primitive and sometimes they were met with suspicion and hostility. They received no favours and very little

The lorry would arrive in the docks for, say 100 sides of beef and the checker would ask him if he wanted some extras. If he was that way inclined he'd take 110, sign for 100 and then, on the way to Smithfield drop the extra lot off at a butcher's shop.
—from *A People's War* by Peter Lewis

left: The last moments of the SS *Tiger*, 2nd April 1942, below: The victory pennants from the periscope of a German U-boat.

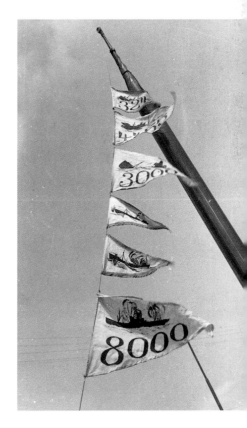

When you could buy sweets they came wrapped in a cone of newspaper like fish and chips did. You tore the newspaper in half afterwards to use in the lavatory.
—from *When I Was Young* by Neil Thomson

### 123 SKIRLY-MIRLY
Boil equal quantities of peeled potatoes and peeled swedes separately in salted water until tender. Drain well. Mash the potatoes and swedes into a smooth paste and mix well. Add a little hot milk and margarine to taste. Season with pepper. Serve piled in a hot vegetable dish.

### LIVER SAVOURY
Chop 1/4 lb (100 g) liver into small pieces, coat them with flour and fry in dripping. Cover 4 slices of stale bread with sliced tomatoes, sprinkle with grated cheese, dot with little lumps of fat and grill quickly. Place the fried liver pieces on top of the grilled bread and serve.

Best was American dried egg. You poured a thin trickle into the frying pan, then as it cooked it blew up like a balloon, till it was two inches thick, like a big yellow hump-backed whale.
—from *Children of the Blitz* by Robert Westall

training, and were expected to carry out the work of the men they were replacing, or augmenting. They worked long hours in seeding, planting and cultivating crops, tending livestock, driving ploughs and tractors (and maintaining them), and bringing in the harvest. Reinforced by German and Italian prisoners-of-war, by conscientious objectors and volunteers, they reached a strength of 200,000, and made a vital contribution to Britain's farming effort. Children, too, were encouraged, during weekends and school holidays, to join "Help a Farmer" schemes.

The "British Restaurants" which had been established in the Blitz for people bombed out of their homes and for transient workers in the target cities, later became a part of urban life, serving one-course meals at a shilling each. By 1943, over 10,000 British Restaurants were providing some 600,000 meals a day. The ambience was austere, the decor non-existent, and self-service was the rule, but the food was nourishing and cost no coupons from the ration book.

Food control in Britain, despite all its complexities and the infinite opportunities it gave for bureaucratic bungling, was well administered. There were some grumbles, as there are bound to be whenever demand exceeds supply, and there was a thriving "black market", in which money could illicitly be used to supplement the ration book, but the scheme, as it evolved, was generally accepted by the public, and it worked. Indeed, it kept on working for a long time after victory was won. Due to world food shortages and adverse weather, British rations of butter, cooking fats and bacon were lower in 1946 than during the war, bread went on the ration, followed by potatoes in 1947. Despite the U-boats, and thanks to the Merchant navies, the British had not starved: in fact, the strict regime had done their health no harm, but it was a happy day, in 1954, when the last ration book was thrown away.

Come and help with the
VICTORY HARVEST

You are needed in the fields !

APPLY TO NEAREST EMPLOYMENT EXCHANGE FOR LEAFLET & ENROLMENT FORM OR WRITE DIRECT TO THE DEPARTMENT OF AGRICULTURE FOR SCOTLAND
15 GROSVENOR STREET, EDINBURGH.

Thousands of men and women who had never seen a ship before poured into the yard to build liberties. Shipyard schools were established to train welders, shipfitters, electricians and joiners. By 1943 the number of shipyard workers reached 700,000, as compared to less than 100,000 during the busiest peacetime years. Salesmen, farmers, students—people who might never have been brought together—all swelled the ranks of shipyard workers. Women, too, signed up in great numbers. At one time, they made up more than 30 percent of the work force at the shipyards. Rosie the Riveter became a popular national image, winding up as Norman Rockwell cover of the *Saturday Evening Post*. Women contributed to all spheres of construction, but most worked as welders, earning themselves another nickname: Wendy the Welder. Women's presence enlivened many work crews, romances flowered and competition between the sexes brought out the best efforts in both. Over 100 liberties were named after women, both the famous and the little known. There were the *Amelia Earhart*, the *Betsy Ross*, the *Dolley Madison*, the *Pocahontas* and the *Emma Lazarus*.
—from *Historic Ships of San Francisco*
by Steven E. Levingston

AMONG AMERICA'S contributions to the Allied cause, her industry's production of cargo ships, and indeed of warships, must stand high upon the list. Even before the United States came into the war, she had provided Britain with sixty Ocean-type cargo ships, and these were soon followed by fifty old and barely seaworthy, but useful "four-pipe" destroyers. Thereafter, the massive expansion of the American ship-building industry was far beyond the capacity of any other country. In 1942, new shipping built for Britain under the auspices of the American Maritime Commission, including ships built for Britain, totalled over 5,000,000 tons, rising to over 12,000,000 tons in 1943.

Eighteen new yards, with a total of 171 shipways, were dedicated by the Commission to the constuction of the so-called "Liberty" EC-2 general cargo ships, each of 7,176 tons gross and 10,500 tons deadweight, with an overall length of 441 feet 7 inches, five cargo holds, a beam of 56 feet 10 inches, a draft (loaded) of 27 feet 7 inches, a range of 17,000 miles and a speed of eleven knots. The normal crew consisted of the master, nine officers, two or three cadets, the bosun, the purser, the carpenter, and forty-eight men. The original design was British, from the Sunderland firm of J.L. Thompson, but the Americans simplified the structure, used many prefabricated parts and replaced riveting with welding. As an example of how welding the hull plates speeded up the process, a 50-way shipyard in 1919 built 69 riveted ships totalling 517,000 deadweight tons, whereas a 12-way Maritime Commission yard in 1943 turned out 205 welded ships 2,150,000 total tons. Each ship contained 121,000 board feet of timber, 72,000 square feet of plywood, a water distillation system, and could carry 440 light tanks or 2,840 Jeeps.

The first Liberty ship, named the *Patrick Henry*, took 244 days to build and, sponsored by Mrs. Henry Wallace, wife of the Vice-President, was launched in Baltimore on 27th September 1941

# LIBERTY SHIPS

President Franklin Delano Roosevelt called it 'the ugly duckling'. 'Ships built by the mile and chopped off by the yard,' as one wag referred to them...the Liberty ships of World War II. Powered by an obsolete reciprocating steam engine that produced 2,500 horse power, the Liberty cruised at 11 knots. The record for speed in assembling a Liberty ship from previously produced components was 4 days, 15 hours.

An American shipyard with 50 ways built 69 riveted ships aggregating 517,000 deadweight tons in 1919. In 1943 a 12-way Maritime Commission yard turned out 205 welded ships totalling 2,150,000 tons.

left: An American Liberty ship being guarded by a British destroyer, HMS *Badsworth,* on 14th April 1943 en route to North Africa.

During World War II, the Liberty ship *Jeremiah O'Brien* operated in both the Atlantic and Pacific theaters, from Omaha Beach to Calcutta. It had been built in East Portland, Maine, in just 57 days, part of the incredible American shipbuilding effort. Today, the *O'Brien* serves as a memorial to all who built and sailed on Liberty ships. 5,601 cargo ships were built during the war, including 2,751 Liberty ships built by 18 American shipyards between 1941 and 1945. More than a quarter of a million men were trained to be seamen and officers of merchant ships. 733 American cargo ships were lost to enemy action and more than 6,000 civilian American seafarers were killed. Thousands were injured during attacks by enemy submarines, aircraft and surface vessels. Many

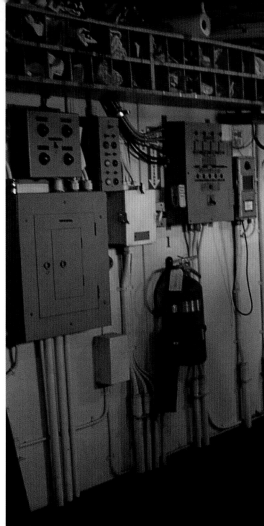

were forced to wait aboard lifeboats and rafts, hoping for rescue after their vessels were lost. Nearly 600 were held as prisoners of war.

The first Liberty ship was named after Patrick Henry. The last 100 were named for merchant seamen who died in wartime service. The first Liberty ship required 244 days to build. By the end of 1945, the average building time for all Liberty shipyards was under 40 days.

all: Images of the SS *Jeremiah O'Brien,* preserved in San Francisco for visitors to see and explore.

## The Liberty ship

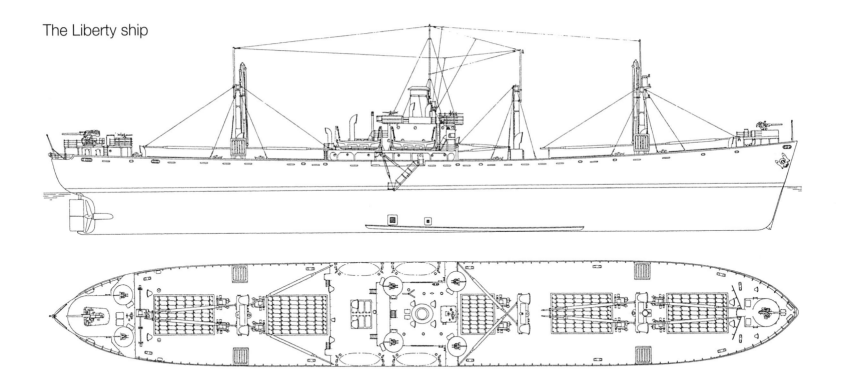

The Maritime Commission in 1937 embarked on a ten-year program to build 500 cargo ships. The cargo ships built between that time and 1st March 1945 include more than 2,500 Liberty ships, about 450 C-type cargo vessels, 550 oceangoing tankers, 175 Victory cargo ships and a variety of military, coastal and smaller craft.

Women workers were 13 per cent of the 700,000 merchant shipyard employees in 1943, and 18 per cent of the 585,000 in October 1944.

and delivered on 31st December. She was to sail 90,000 miles, and to carry 110,000 tons of cargo in every theatre of war except the Asiatic. On the run to Murmansk, she was targeted by aircraft and by U-boats, but escaped; later, off North Africa, she suffered bomb and bullet damage, but throughout her life at sea she never needed a major overhaul of hull or machinery.

By 1944 the average time for the construction of a Liberty ship had been reduced to 42 days, and 140 vessels were being launched every month. By then, women formed 18 per cent of the work force, forty skilled trades were involved in the process, and 36,000 houses, costing $40,000,000, were put up around the shipyards to accommodate the workers.

The Liberty ships were not the most beautiful of vessels (President Roosevelt once described them

as "dreadful-looking objects"), but their cost— $2,000,000 per hull—was low, and their prefabricated parts and welded plates made them particularly suitable for mass assembly. Furthermore, they came along at exactly the right time—a time when Britain's shipping losses were exceeding her capacity for replacement.

Of the industrialists who set up assembly plants throughout the USA to turn out the Liberty ships, and who vied with one another to produce the most, perhaps the best known was Henry J. Kaiser, a Californian civil engineer who knew all there was to know about building dams and bridges but, it was rumoured, could neither tell port from starboard nor stem from stern. His expertise lay in the field of mass production, and, as a result of his and other shipyard owners' efforts, by October 1945, when the last, the *Albert M. Boe* (named after a chief engineer who had died a hero's death at sea), was delivered, 2,751 Liberty ships had been built in Maritime Commission yards. These were in addition to 450 C-type cargo ships, 550 T-2 or T-3 ocean-going tankers and, beginning in February 1944, over 300 VC-2 "Victory" general cargo ships.

The Victory ships were built to a Maritime Commission design, and although they were slightly larger than the Liberty ships, they took even less time to construct. Powered by turbines instead of steam engines, they were 50 per cent faster and had a slightly longer range. After the first, the United Victory, whose service life was spent in the Pacific theatre, thirty-five Victory ships were named for the allied nations and the rest for towns, cities, universities and colleges in the USA.

At the height of the construction programme, one Liberty ship, the *Robert G. Peary* (most Liberty ships were named after prominent American citizens), was completed within four days and fifteen-and-a-half hours of her keel being laid, and was fitted out ready for sailing three days later. One lady who had been invited to christen one of the Liberty ships, was standing ready for the launching with a champagne bottle in her hand when she noticed that the keel had yet to be laid. She enquired of Henry Kaiser what he thought she ought to do. "Just start swinging, Ma'am," he replied.

The American *Christopher Newport* was one of seven Liberty ships in the ill-fated convoy PQ17 which set out from Iceland for Murmansk on 27th June 1942. Patrolling U-boats first made contact with the convoy on 2nd July, some 60 miles west of Bear Island, but their attacks were repulsed by the strong destroyer escort. Later in the day, eight torpedo-bombers were also driven off and, on the next day, twenty-six more were frustrated by low cloud. In the early hours of 4th July, a Heinkel 115 appeared out of the fog which lay like a blanket

above the mastheads of the convoy, and aimed a torpedo at the anti-aircraft ship *Palomares*, before climbing steeply back into the overcast. The anti-aircraft ships' siren sounded six piercing blasts to indicate a sudden change of course. The torpedo ran along *Palomares*' side, passed between two ships in the convoy's outer column, hit the *Christopher Newport* and exploded in her engine room, killing the 3rd Engineer and two greasers. One of her newly-trained gunners, Seaman 1st Class Hugh P. Wright, manning a 0.3 machine gun on the flying bridge, had seen the torpedo coming and directed an accurate stream of fire at it until the explosion blew him off the bridge. The ship was abandoned, the first of 22 merchantmen to be lost by PQ17. Her 47 survivors, including Seaman Wright, were quickly picked up by the crew of the rescue ship *Zamalek*, who were surprised to find that most of them were black, smartly dressed in shore-going clothes, remarkably cheerful and of ages which ranged from eighteen to eighty.

A well-built vessel, the *Christopher Newport* did not sink, and there were those who thought she ought to have been salvaged, but the naval commander of the close escort considered that the time taken to take her in tow would have endangered others of his charges, and he ordered one of his submarines, *P614*, to sink her. She survived, however, the "friendly" torpedoes and two depth-charges from the corvette HMS *Dianella*, and only succumbed when Korvettenkäpitan Brandenburg, commanding *U457*, attracted to the scene by the sound of detonations on his hydrophone, sent her to the bottom of the Barents Sea with 10,000 tons of war supplies she was carrying to Russia.

In the annals of the Liberty ships, a story to be hallowed is of the *Henry Bacon*—one of over thirty merchantmen, mostly American, which were assembling off Murmansk on 17th February 1945 for the return voyage to Britain as convoy RA64. It

above: A wartime U.S. Navy sweetheart handkerchief, right: A German propaganda leaflet.

so happened that, a few days earlier, some 500 Norwegians—the entire population of Soroya Island, a few miles west of North Cape—had come under attack by a force of Germans, and four British destroyers from Polyarno had been assigned to rescue them. The evacuation was faultlessly carried out, and the refugees were apportioned among the convoy ships. Sixty-five were put aboard the *Henry Bacon*.

For one reason or another, the convoy was slow in forming up and, during the delay, one of the escort sloops, HMS *Lark*, was put out of action by a U-boat's Gnat torpedo. Naval efforts to aid the

Danger ahead !

Australia to San Francisco. She supported the D-Day invasions in 1944 by making eleven shuttle trips between England and the Normandy beaches. In 1946, she completed her final voyage and was laid up in the reserve fleet at Suisin Bay near San Francisco. In 1979, after dodging the scrap man for 33 years, she was designated as a memorial ship and steamed to San Francisco for restoration. Open daily as a museum, she makes two cruises around San Francisco Bay annually. She is berthed at Pier 32. In 1994, the *O'Brien* returned to the D-Day beaches and to several ports in England, France and East Coast of the US. The 17,000 mile voyage took five months. She was the only ship of the original 5,000 ship D-Day armada to return for the commemoration 50 years later.

stricken sloop depleted the convoy's defences at a crucial moment, and another Liberty ship, the *Thomas Scott*, was blown in two by a torpedo. Her crew and 41 Norwegian passengers, were rescued by the destroyer *Onslaught*, and at last RA64 emerged into the open Barents Sea and set course north-west. Keeping well clear of the destroyer escort, six U-boats followed in pursuit.

By the evening of 18th February, a full gale was blowing, the seas were mountainous, the merchantmen were widely scattered, and to reassemble them called for a major effort by the destroyers, all running low on fuel and prevented by the weather from approaching the oilers. Early next morning, the first of many Ju-88 torpedo-bombers was seen approaching from the south-west. An article in the Norwegian magazine "Western Viking" describes the scene:

"The worst storm of the entire northern campaign struck this convoy and severely damaged the *Henry Bacon*. The *Bacon* had many Norwegians on board when she was disabled and found by German torpedo planes, but the odds caught up with them and the *Bacon* was mortally wounded. There was only room for so many in the lifeboat, and even in times of war it was women

The Henry J. Kaiser shipyard in Richmond, California completed its first Liberty ship in 197 days. In August 1942 the Kaiser yard in Portland, Oregon turned out the Liberty *Pierre S. DuPont* in 31 days. The Richmond yard then finished the *Joseph W. Teal* in 16 days. But the record effort went to the Kaiser gang that assembled the *Robert E. Peary* in just 4 days, 15 hours.

Named and freshly painted wartime gray, a Liberty ship still did not take aboard a single bag of grain or round of ammunition until it passed a series of rigid seaworthiness tests. The Maritime Commission's trial board went for a two-day outing with throttles opened wide. A full crew demonstrated the ship's readiness by spinning her wheel on a dizzying course, swinging her in circles, running her astern full speed. All the while trial board members combed the ship from forepeak to poop, listening to her purr, testing her fuel consumption, her horsepower, surveying her holds, inspecting her equipment, pipes, wiring, and safety devices.
—from *Historic Ships of San Francisco*
by Steven E. Levingston

**Typical World War II Liberty Ship Crew**
**Master, Chief Mate,** Second Mate, Third Mate, Radio Officer, Deck Cadet, Bosun, Carpenter, Able-Seamen (6), Ordinary Seamen (3), Purser, **Gunnery Officer,** Petty Officer, Signalman, Gunners (18),
**Chief Engineer,** 1st Assistant Engineer, 2nd Assistant Engineer, 3rd Assistant Engineer, Engine Cadet, Deck Engineer, Oilers (3), Firemen/Watertenders (3), Wipers (2), **Chief Steward,** Chief Cook, 2nd Cook & Baker, Messmen Deck (3), Bedroom Stewards (3), Scullery (2).

and children first. All of the Norwegians were put in the boat and saved. Many of the crew of the *Henry Bacon*, including the Captain and Chief Engineer, gave up their places in the boat so that the refugees might survive. They knew without question that they were going to perish with their ship in the Arctic Sea."

The escort carrier HMS *Nairana*'s Wildcat fighters, operating from a wildly-pitching deck and frequently harassed by "friendly" anti-aircraft fire, nevertheless succeeded in destroying six Ju-88s. Other German pilots flew back to their bases with exaggerated claims of ships damaged or destroyed. In fact, all but two of those which had set out from Kola had reached safe anchorage by 1st March—the worst-battered in the Faroes (with the Norwegian refugees), and the remainder in the Clyde. The *Henry Bacon* was the last Allied ship to be sunk by German aircraft in World War II, and the conduct of her crew was in the highest and noblest traditions of the sea.

Jeremiah O'Brien was the commander of the First American Naval Flying Squadron of the War of the Revolution, and his name was given to a Liberty ship constructed for the War Shipping Administration at South Portland, Maine, and launched on 19th June 1943. She sailed on four Atlantic convoys, made eleven shuttle trips between England and the American invasion beaches during Operation Overlord, and ended her war in the Pacific. In 1946, with hundreds of other wartime vessels, she was consigned to a "reserve fleet", much of which was sold, scrapped or sunk as the years went by. The *O'Brien* survived, as was her habit, and when the National Liberty Ship Memorial, Inc. was formed in 1978 to find and preserve an original Liberty ship, she was there to meet the need.

Now, when not away on her annual cruise, she is open to the public at Pier 32 in San Francisco. Wartime slogans hang upon the walls of her engine room and cabins; Loose lips might sink ships and Alert! Your skill and devotion will win the war. Only two Liberty ships survive today: the *John W. Brown*, based on the East Coast of the U.S., and the *O'Brien*. The *Jeremiah O'Brien* was the only operational survivor of the 5,000 ships which formed the Overlord armada, to sail to Normandy in 1994. Aboard was a wartime Admiral and many veterans, to take part in the ceremonies commemorating the 50th anniversary of the D-Day landings.

On building the Liberty ships at the Henry J. Kaiser yard in Richmond, California in 1943: A procession of tin hats, overalls and lunch boxes, crowding into a new world—piles of steel plates of all shapes and sizes, shacks and booths, ladders and scaffolds, posters like the one reminding you that the guy who relaxes is helping the Axis. The yard was arranged city-like: F, G, H streets running in one direction, 9th, 10th, 11th streets in another. It was a city without houses, but the traffic was heavy. Cranes, trucks, trains noised by. Finally, after a rather long walk, I came to the edge of the water. There were the ships—or rather, halves, thirds, quarters and tenths of ships. There was a piece of ship here and a piece of ship there, and a hole in between. And then out of a clear blue sky a crane dropped the missing piece of ship, big as a house, into that hole.
—from *Swing Shift* by Joseph Fabry

The SS *Jeremiah O'Brien* made seven voyages in WWII including four to Europe and eleven shuttle trips between England and the Normandy beaches.

(the Liberty Ship) is accredited with saving not only Britain, not only the Allied cause, but the whole world from disaster—for there was a grave fear that the war might be lost simply because Allied lifelines were stretched beyond the limit owing to an insufficient number of ships.
—from *The Liberty Ships* by Leonard Sawyer

The S.S. *Elihu Yale* left New York harbor 12/14/43 for Norfolk, Virginia where she left in a 70-ship convoy, arriving in Oran, Algeria on 1/11/44. From there, she sailed to Augusta, Sicily on 2/3/44 and on the 8th, she sailed to Naples, Italy. She departed Naples on the 12th, arriving at Anzio on 2/13/44 with 40 U.S. Navy Armed Guard, 45 Merchant Seamen and 180 Army personnel on board to discharge the cargo. From the time she arrived at the beachhead at 0840 on the 13th, to the time she was hit, there were frquent air raids and almost a constant

shelling of the waters around her by long range coastal guns. At approximately 1811, Feb. 15, 1944, they were notified via radio that an air alert was in progress. This was the 15th or 16th alert since 0900 the same day and it gave the position of the planes as 8 miles north of Anzio—10 miles north of where the *Yale* was anchored. The general quarters alarm was rung, the gun crew went to their battle stations, the shore batteries opened fire and at 1812 a terrific explosion shook the ship as the bomb hit the after part of number 4 hatch. The bomb was identified by several members of the gun crew as a glider bomb. The bomb blew up the main deck and folded it back against the after gun platform, carrying with it the aft mast, deck locker and the number 7 and number 8 MM gun tubs—leaving a hole just above the waterline the width of the ship and extending from the midships deckhouse to number 5 hatch. At the time, the ship was about 40 percent discharged. Number 4 hold was empty—the other four were partially filled with gasoline, ammunition and some general cargo. The fire broke out immediately as the fuel oil tanks were ignited and it spread to the LCT loaded with ammunition which was tied on the Port Side aft,

discharging the number 5 hold. The fire later gutted the entire midships deckhouse. The ship's powerplant was wrecked by the explosion; consequently, it was impossible to get water on deck with which to fight the fire. The number 7 20MM was firing at the time the bomb hit and afterwards; several other 20MM guns and the forward 3" 50 fired for a minute ot two at enemy aircraft until out of range. Due to the raging fire, the LCT exploding shells in all directions, the danger of a subsequent explosion of the cargo and their inability to fight the fire, it was decided that the ship was to be abandoned in order to save as many lives as possible. The Captain ordered the ship abandoned at approximately 1820. The Navy gun crew stationed amidships and forward were ordered to leave the ship as there were no enemy aircraft over the area and nothing could be done to save the ship. The gunners on the aft gun platforms, who were cut off from the rest of the ship, were ordered by the coxswain to leave the ship because of the exploding ammunition. The number 1 lifeboat, two large rafts forward and numerous doughnut rafts were put over the side (the other lifeboats, etc. were destroyed) and the men went down ropes and

ladders into them. In so far as possible, the ship was searched for wounded personnel and they were lowered down into the lifeboats and rafts. The ship was finally completely abandoned about 1915, the last person going over the side onto the USS *SC-690* which pulled alongside of the starboard bow. The men from all boats and rafts landed at the beach, or were taken aboard SCs and LCTs. A few hours later, at the request of Captain Turner, British N.O.I.C., the Captain of the S.S. *Elihu Yale*, T.W. Ekstrom, three Navy Officers and 8 members of the Merchant Crew returned to the ship and boarded it but could do practically nothing as the fire was still burning in the midships deckhouse. They did secure all confidential publications which were not already destroyed and they were turned over to the Captain of the USS *Hopi*, a salvage tug which was fighting the fire. These men stayed aboard the *Hopi* that night and returned back on board the *Yale* the next morning. The ship was still smoldering and the midship deckhouse was completely gutted. The S.S. *Elihu Yale* settled on the bottom in about 35 feet of water and had started to split in half at number 4 hatch.
—Roger P. Wise, D-V(S), USN

...sailing aboard a Liberty offered considerable comfort. The officers' and crew's quarters were all in one house, eliminating the need for men to pass over weather decks to reach messes. Officers were able to retreat to private rooms; crewmen slept two or three to a room. Officers and crew ate at separate sittings, the officers in the "saloon", the crew in another dining area. And one luxury for all were the showers, a great leap forward from the merchant seaman's traditional bucket-washings.

—from *Historic Ships of San Francisco* by Steven E. Levingston

above: Wrens working in the Operations Plotting Room at the Naval Services Headquarters, Ottawa, December 1943.

A FULL TWO YEARS before World War II began, preparations had been put in hand to provide the merchantmen with paravanes (an anti-mine device trailed on the beam), and with deck armament to meet the threat of U-boats. There had been no shortage of volunteers to man the guns, and training courses for them were being run in several British ports. By the end of 1939, 1,500 guns had been mounted on merchant ships, and the vessels' fabric strengthened to support them and withstand their recoil; most of the guns, however, were of WWI vintage, and were only capable of firing at low elevations. There was a serious shortage of weapons for defence against air attack. The few available Lewis light machine guns had to be switched from ship to ship as one came into port and another sailed. On one occasion, a seaman, furious at the feeling of impotence, hurled a grenade at a low-flying attacking aircraft, and scored a bullseye on its fuselage. It was a brave effort, which could only have been bettered if he had remembered to remove the firing pin.

From the beginning of the WWII, Germany made widespread use of a British invention which dated from the first war. This was the magnetic mine, of which large numbers were "sown" by U-boats in British coastal waters, and by aircraft in harbour mouths and estuaries. Approximately one in every four mines laid caused damage, and many merchant ships were sunk. An Admiralty team had been examining the problem for some time, but it was not until an unexploded mine, dropped by parachute off Shoeburyness in November 1939, was hauled ashore and taken to pieces (with courage and great care) that the appropriate counter-measures were devised. The first, and simplest, was to detonate the mines at a safe distance, but there were not enough mine-sweepers to carry out the task. Another measure was to de-magnetise or "degauss" a ship (gauss being the unit of magnetic induction) by passing an electric current through copper cables wrapped

below: Bill Hudson, whose CAM ship *Empire Lawrence* was attacked and sunk by enemy aircraft as it sailed in convoy PQ16 en route to Murmansk in May 1942, left: *Canada's Answer* by Norman Wilkinson.

"I believe the only time we were really afraid was when the ship's engines broke down and the convoy just sailed on and left us. A ship with no power is like a tomb. There's an unearthly silence, and every hammer blow, every sound of something falling in the engine room, sounds like thunder and makes everyone jump. The ship around the hull.

By the spring of 1940, 2,000 merchant ships and 1,704 warships had been de-gaussed, but there were 10,000 vessels on Lloyd's Register alone, and enormous lengths of cable would have been required had not a Naval Mines Department scientist suggested that the same effect could be achieved by using a temporary coil to pass a very powerful current through the ship, and so neutralise its magnetic field. This process came to known as "wiping", and the knowledge that his ship had been thoroughly "wiped" convinced the majority of seamen that they were safe, at least from the magnetic mine.

In the early years of the war, few self-respecting Navy men wanted to be assigned to convoy duties, and in the warships' wardrooms, noses were turned up at the very notion of specialising in anti-submarine activity. After all, who would not rather do battle with the *Bismarck* or the *Tirpitz* than trudge across the oceans with a lot of tramps and tankers? One of the few to see a future in it was 1st Lieutenant (later Rear-Admiral) Philip Burnett, who began the war as Lord Louis Mountbatten's No. 1 on the destroyer HMS *Kelly*. Burnett became the chief instructor at the Navy's anti-submarine school and, in 1943, took command of a Canadian Escort Group at a time when the Royal Canadian Navy was making a substantial impact in the North Atlantic. By then, attitudes were changing. The Battle of the Atlantic took on a certain glamour, and began to offer a

below: Tribal Class destroyers *Haida* and *Athabaskan*, on manoeuvres in the English Channel, right: At the wheel of a merchant ship in a Malta convoy, 21st August 1942, overleaf: *Queen Mary Raising Steam* by Norman Wilkinson

just lies there, with no leeway, responding to the motion of the sea. Our hearts were in our mouths, knowing how sound, travelling through water, could be picked up by a U-boat. Sometimes we were immobile for twenty-four hours, and there was immense relief when the ship was under way again and belting along at maximum speed to catch up with the convoy and get a 'Welcome back' signal from the Commodore."
—Jack Armstrong, steward, Merchant Navy

fashionable arena. Thereafter, commands in the Western Approaches were eagerly sought after.

Able Seaman Thomas Rowe recalls an attack by German aircraft on the coaster *Empire Daffodil* as she sailed up the Channel bound for the Port of London on 9th July 1940. "We were light ship, having discharged our cargo at Plymouth. The sea was calm, and we were sailing alone in brilliant sunshine, when we were suddenly attacked by ME-109s, diving out of the sun. I manned the Holman projector and fired the missiles until our supply ran out. Apart from the machine-gun on the wing of the bridge there was nothing else to hit back with. We managed to avoid the bombs dropped by the aircraft, but the hull was punctured several times by armour-piercing bullets, and the ship began to take in water. We got into Weymouth harbour just as the tide was running out and settled in the mud. Royal Navy engineers came out and welded metal plates over the lowest holes, which enabled us to sail into harbour on the next full tide and get the repairs completed."

In March 1941, after Field Marshal Erwin Rommel's lightning campaign in Cyrenaica, Wavell's Eighth Army held Tobruk like a fortress encircled by the enemy, and even that precarious toe-hold on the shore of North Africa would have been impossible but for the supplies and reinforcements brought in by the Merchant Navy. When at last the Africa Corps took the fortress, it was the merchant ships which played the major part in the evacuation, as it had done after the collapse of Greece in two short weeks, which put 58,000 British troops at risk of death or capture, and when Crete, too, soon fell to the enemy.

On 27th April 1941, the *City of London* weighed anchor in Kalamata Bay with over 3,000 troops aboard, most of them Australian, and set course for Alexandria. That afternoon, a Scottish soldier came on deck, produced the inevitable bagpipes, and commenced the process of putting them in tune. A recumbent Bren gunner propped himself up on an elbow and voiced a protest. "Give me bloody dive-bombing every time," he proclaimed.

From the beginning of April until 20th May 1941, twenty-five British merchantmen, totalling over 140,000 tons, were sunk, most of them by bombing, in the pleasant, blue waters of the Mediterranean. For many months thereafter,

When we were somewhere between Port Moresby and Darwin, news came through that the bomb had been dropped on Hiroshima and then on Nagasaki. Early one morning after that, the chap on lookout on the bridge came down into the Mess, woke everybody up, and said the war was over, for which he was abused and accused of pulling our legs. Confirmation of his truthfulness came when he produced a bottle of whisky from the Captain. To get a bottle like that so easy, the war *had* to be over. As we left Darwin, VJ-Day was declared, and all the ships in harbour were dressed overall with sirens blowing.
—E. Withers, ex-DEMS gunner, Merchant Navy

indeed until the Allies were established in Sicily and on the toe of Italy, the Merchant Navy provided the lifeline for the Allied forces in the Middle East.

There were times when a merchantman, alone on the high seas, was caught by a U-boat on patrol. Then, the master had to choose between defiance and surrender. A Type VIIC U-boat, moving on the surface, could make more than 17 knots, and few cargo ships could equal that. But if the merchantman put up enough of a fight to persuade the U-boat commander to submerge, that cut its speed by more than half, and there might be a chance of making a run for it. Many a rookie gun-crew fought it out with a U-boat's gunners and, at least for a while, gave as good as they got; many a chief engineer screwed down the safety valves and opened up the taps to maintain his top speed plus a little more; many a helmsman spotted the rippling wake of a torpedo, and took effective evasive action; many a radio operator stayed staunchly at his set, tapping out a call for help while the battle raged around him. The sad fact was that, unless a friendly destroyer or aircraft was in range and could answer the call, the U-boat was almost sure to win the fight.

The second time that Thomas Rowe came under fire was in 1942, when the Great Lakes steamer *Fred W. Green*, bound for Freetown from Bermuda, was attacked in the late evening of 31st May. "Shells smashed into the ship, and into our deck cargo of motor vehicles, which exploded when their petrol tanks were hit. I got away on the one remaining lifeboat. The U-boat, *U506*, came alongside, and the commander asked what ship we were, what cargo we were carrying, and where we were bound. I heard later that *U506* was sunk by aircraft of Vigo."

In 1943, Britain's operational research people examined the relationship between convoy size and losses, and they found that, in 1942 and 43,

the larger convoys, of 40 ships or more, had suffered lower per centage losses than those of fewer numbers. They also calculated that the length of a big convoy's perimeter did not increase in proportion with its numbers, and that, if six escorts were needed for a 40 ship convoy, seven were sufficient for one of twice the size. There was the additional consideration that an 80 ship convoy sailing every fortnight could carry the same tonnage of freight as one of 40 ships sailing every week. It meant more problems at assembly points, at the ports of loading and discharge, and more grey hairs for the Commodores: more importantly, it meant more cargoes getting through to their destinations.

Next, the escort tactics came under scrutiny. The principles of warfare held good for the sea as much as for the land and for the air, and although "concentration of effort" came high on the list in the early days of the Atlantic battle, it took a while for the Navy to implement the local superiority of force. Captain Frederick "Johnny" Walker, the champion escort group leader in the North Atlantic, understood this doctrine and practised it with great success. Once the Asdic operator in Walker's sloop HMS *Starling*, or in one of his ships, identified the sonar echo of a U-boat, it was rare for the U-boat to escape. Churchill himself was persuaded that offensive patrols by such groups as "Walker's chicks", as they were known in Liverpool, paid better dividends than simply shepherding the convoys.

A torpedo might strike home with a sickening thud that shook the ship, make a vast explosion and throw up a towering plume of water, but, if it missed the engine room, it might not have dealt a fatal blow. It would make a great hole below the water-line, but that did not mean the ship would sink, at least, not straightaway. A load of good Canadian timber could keep a ship afloat for days, and holes could be blocked to some extent, if not

Most casualties at sea are actually the result of panic, which is the produce of ignorance. In a life-or-death emergency you are not going to be entirely free of panic.
*Don't* depend on peacetime experience and regulations. Keep your eye out for recent and current bulletins issued by the Marine Inspection Service, which has gathered a large amount of data and from it proposed many improvements and changes in safety and lifeboat regulations. *Don't* depend on what is in the lifeboat.
*Don't* stint yourself on

above: A U-boat lookout stands his four-hour watch, below: A Type VII crosses the Bay of Biscay, far right: An exhausted U-boat crewman catches a nap in the forward torpedo room.

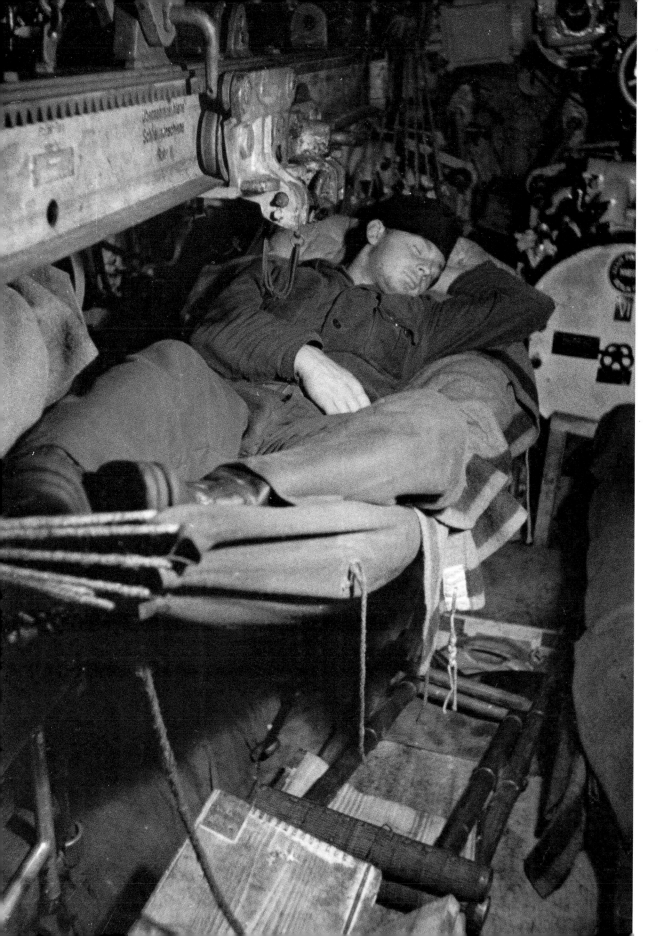

safety gear for your own protection. Steamship operators are like all other businessmen—except for providing five thousand dollars insurance on each seaman, from the captain to the messboy. They wish to keep expenses at a minimum. So if the steamship operator does not do the supplying, you yourself do the buying. A few dollars from your pocket may mean all the difference between your becoming a 1943 casualty or a 1983 veteran.

*Don't* let human nature trick you into indifference. A man will readily pay for comfort and a good appearance; but he is reluctant to part with dollars to protect his most precious possession—his own life. The reason for this indifference is plain. He is constantly aware of the benefits of comfort and a good appearance, but death is beyond his experience. He cannot identify himself with it. Death is something that happens to the other fellow.

—from *HOW TO ABANDON SHIP* by Phil Richards and John J. Banigan

right: A U-boat takes on provisions in a flooded dry-dock at one of the Biscay ports, below: a similar drydock at Saint Nazaire in 1996.

A great roar went up from the men on the upper deck, a howl of triumph. The U-boat came up bows first at an extraordinary angle, blown right out of her proper trim by the force of the explosion: clearly she was, for the

moment, beyond control. The water sluiced and poured from her casings as she rose: great bubbles burst round her conning tower: gouts of oil spread outwards from the crushed plating amidships. "Open fire!" shouted Ericson—and for a few moments it was Baker's chance, and his alone: the two-pounder pom-pom, set just behind the funnel, was the only gun that could be brought to bear. The staccato force of its firing shook the still air, and with a noise and a chain of shock like the punch! punch! punch! of a trip-hammer the red glowing tracer-shells began to chase each other low across the water towards the U-boat. She had now fallen back on a level keel, and for the moment she rode at her proper trim: it was odd, and infinitely disgusting, suddenly to see this wicked object, the loathsome cause of a hundred nights of fear and disaster, so close to them, so innocently exposed. It was like seeing some criminal, who had outraged honour and society, and had long been shunned, taking his ease at one's own fireside.
—from *THE CRUEL SEA* by Nicholas Monsarrat

# A FEW CARELESS WORDS MAY END IN THIS—

Many lives were lost in the last war through careless talk
Be on your guard! Don't discuss movements of ships or troops

During the past 3 1/2 years, the Navy has been dependent upon the Merchant Marine to supply our far-flung fleet and bases. Without this support, the Navy could not have accomplished its mission. Consequently, it is fitting that the Merchant Marine share in our success as it shared in our trials. The Merchant Marine is a strong bulwark of national defense in peace and war, and a buttress to a sound national economy. A large Merchant Marine is not only an important national resource; it is, in being, an integral part of the country's armed might during time of crisis. During World War II, this precept had been proven. As the Merchant Marine returns to its peacetime pursuits, I take pleasure in expressing the Navy's heartfelt thanks to you and through you to the officers and men of the Merchant Marine for their magnificent support during World War II. All hands can feel pride of accomplishment in a job well done. We wish the Merchant Marine every success during the years ahead and sincerely hope that it remains strong and continues as a vital and integral part of our national economy and defense.
—Fleet Admiral Ernest J. King, Commander in Chief, United States Navy and Chief of Naval Operations

far left: Firing a Mk II depth charge thrower from HMCS *Pictou*, left: Under attack in a Malta convoy, above left: Bofors gun maintenance en route to Malta, above: Flak-filled sky over this Malta-bound convoy under air attack.

On 9th July 1940 I was serving aboard the coaster *Empire Daffodil*, sailing up the English Channel bound for the London river. We were light ship having discharged our cargo at Plymouth. The sea was calm in brilliant sunshine and we were sailing alone. Aircraft were heard overhead and suddenly we were attacked by German Messerschmitt 109s diving at us from out of the sun. I manned the Holman Ejector and fired our missiles into the air in order to keep the enemy aircraft away, until our supply of missiles ran out. Apart from the machine gun that was being fired from the wing of the bridge, we had nothing else to hit back with. The ship managed to avoid all the bombs that the aircraft dropped but our hull was punctured several times by armour-piercing bullets and the ship began to take on water. However, we managed to get into Weymouth harbour just as the tide was running out and the ship settled on the mud. Royal Navy engineers came out and welded metal plates over the lowest shell holes which enabled us to sail in to harbour on the next full tide, where the repairs were accomplished.
—Thomas Rowe, Ordinary Seaman

The life-line is firm
thanks to the
MERCHANT NAVY

left: Provisioning a lifeboat on the motor vessel *Empire Unity* in 1942, below: A sing-song in the dog watches on *Empire Unity*.

A pretty young woman asked me if I were interested in meeting and staying with a family for a night. It was such a wonderful opportunity and I agreed without hesitation. I took the address and directions to the home which was out of the city, and after a short bus ride arrived at their doorstep. They invited me in and served me some tea and biscuits. That evening we enjoyed a delicious but spare dinner of meat pie, potatoes, bread and tea. We then set about talking about the terrible war and the young men "such as yourself" who were involved. I retired for the night in the comfort of their home. In the morning, breakfast was ready, consisting of an egg, some toast and marmalade and tea. I bade them goodbye and returned to the ship where I told my shipmates of my evening and of breakfast. "You what?" yelled one of the fellows. "You ate their egg! Goddammit, they only get about one egg a month and you ate it. You stupid son of a bitch." I was at a loss and felt so guilty and full of remorse, and yet it was too late to do anything about it.
—Thom Hendrickson, DEMS Signalman, U.S.N.

right: War brides arriving in Canada on the *Queen Mary.*

repaired. Ships travelled far, and sometimes reached their destinations (perhaps helped by a tow-line or two), with all sorts of damage down below. When the *Carsbreck*, for example, sailing with the ill-fated convoy SC7 on 17th October 1940, was torpedoed by Heinrich Liebe's *U38*, she went down by the head and listed heavily to port, but her load of timber kept her up, and, steaming at 5 knots, she struggled on and docked in Liverpool. Sadly, she was one of three ships of convoy HG75 to be sunk by *U564* one year later on 24th October 1941 in the North Atlantic.

Canada's vital contribution to the Battle of the Atlantic was crucial in terms of the administration of the major port at Halifax, of liaison between Britain and America, of the essential provision of reconnaissance aircraft, escort ships and personnel, and particularly in the construction and operation of corvettes.

There are official charts on which the position of every merchant ship sunk by a U-boat during certain phases of the war is marked by a little cross. For the period April 1940 to March 1941, the crosses stretch from the Faroes, past the southern coast of Iceland, through the Western Approaches (where they lie thick), down past the Spanish coast, the Azores and the western coast of Africa to Freetown. To study such a chart is to feel a shudder of dismay, and to turn to the chart for August 1942 to May 1943 is to be sickened and appalled. By the end of 1943, however, the picture had significantly improved, with the advent of the hunter-killer escort groups, the long-range aircraft with the latest search radar, now operating from the Azores as well as from Britain, Iceland and the Americas. The "air gap" in the Atlantic had been filled, and the losses in November were the lowest since May 1940.

OF ALL THE PRODUCTS Britain needed for survival in the early 1940s, let alone to fight the war, oil was crucial, and every gallon had to come from overseas, so the role of her tanker fleets, and those of friendly nations, was absolutely vital to the Allied cause. The large peacetime supplies from the East and Middle East had reached Britain through the Suez Canal and the Mediterranean—a route which from June 1940 was virtually closed. Winston Churchill faced the fact that Britain needed the capacity of four large tankers every day: "I trust steps are being taken," he instructed the Secretary for Petroleum, "to draw as much oil as possible from America, thus avoiding the long haul from the Persian Gulf round the Cape."

The tankers *Regent Tiger* and *Kennebec*, sunk by U-boats in the Western Approaches, were two of twenty-five merchant vessels to be lost in the first three weeks of war. From then on, the officers and men of the major oil carriers—Anglo-Saxon Petroleum (Shell), Anglo-American (Esso), British Oil, British Tankers, Bulk Oil, Eagle Oil, Northern Petroleum and Oriental—were in the thick of the Atlantic battle, and they were carrying the most dangerous of cargoes. Ships loaded with wheat, meat and iron ore might be holed and sunk, might turn over, catch on fire, but they would rarely burn like furnaces until they exploded, turning the sea into a blazing cauldron in which a quick death by drowning was a merciful release.

On 12th August 1940, the 8,000 ton tanker *British Fame*, sailing with convoy OB193 between Madeira and the Azores, earned the dubious distinction of becoming the first vessel of the war to be sunk by an Italian submarine. The successful *Malaspia* was one of the 27-strong Atlantic Flotilla which il Duce, Benito Mussolini, had placed under Admiral Dönitz's command at Bordeaux.

Captain George Waite of Eagle Oil had the worst of luck. It was as though fate had chosen him to meet disaster after disaster. In December 1939, his *San Alberto*, outward bound for Trinidad, had been torpedoed and sunk 140 miles south of Fastnet. Eleven months later, he gave the order to abandon the blazing *San Demetrio* when the *Admiral Scheer* attacked convoy HX84 in the Western Approaches, and the *Jervis Bay* fought to the end, like a mother chicken defending her brood. On 15th June 1943, Waite was to be master of the *San Ernesto*, in ballast for Bahrein from Sydney, when she was torpedoed by Japanese submarine *I31* and also had to be abandoned.

Tankers, however, occasionally demonstrated a degree of survivability denied to other ships. The derelict *San Ernesto* drifted for 2,000 miles before she ran aground, and the famous story of the *San Demetrio* epitomises the bravery and endurance of the merchant seamen at war. Her crew, too, had engaged the *Admiral Scheer* with their only gun, but it was a hopeless gesture. While star-shells lit the evening sky, two shots from the *Scheer*'s big guns hit the tanker. Her flying bridge was broken, her navigation bridge a mass of tangled iron, her bows and well-decks were holed, there was damage in her boiler room and engine room, and she was ablaze. Captain Waite put his confidential papers in a weighted bag and threw it overboard, and all but three of her crew got clear in the lifeboats, which lost contact in the night with each other and with the *San Demetrio*. The sixteen men in one lifeboat saw the Swedish steamer *Stureholm* in the distance, picking up survivors from the *Jervis Bay*, and tried but failed to catch the rescuer's attention.

Taking turns at the oars, they rowed the lifeboat for two days in rain and heavy seas, but such were the winds and motion of the waves that, on the second day, they found themselves still in sight of the tanker which was afire and pouring smoke. They pulled towards her, and there was some discussion as to whether they should board her (she was carrying 11,200 tons of petrol). It was an American apprentice seaman, Oswald Preston,

"I enjoyed being on tankers. The conditions were better than on the freighters, and so was the food. The downside was that we berthed at oil installations, well away from town and city centres, and when we got to port, discharge only took a day. But when we had the chance, we lived life to the full, and our motto was 'Live each day as though it were your last'.
—Jack Armstrong, tanker steward, Merchant Navy

Swim, wounded and bomb-shocked, through flaming oil which clogs throat and nostrils and scorches everything it touches, to a bullet-riddled boat. In that very precarious refuge, whilst an equally dazed and damaged shipmate scoops the viscous filth from your breathing passages, watch the ship you have fought through thousands of leagues of danger—man-made and elemental—break apart and plunge sullenly to the bottom of the sea it has gallantly defied for years. Remember, as you play spectator to such a shameful tragedy, that in all probability, your best friends lie mangled and dead among the twisted wreckage. These dead men

cheered you on when the battle for existence seemed too fierce to allow of any hope. They taught you the trade of the sea, and showed you the sea's mysteries and immensities.
—from *The Merchant Navy at War* by Capt. Frank H. Shaw

below: The *San Demetrio,* a tanker attacked and set ablaze by enemy raiders, was saved by the heroic efforts of Chief Engineer Charles Pollard and other crew members.

known to the crew as "Yank", who decided the issue when he said that he would rather fry than freeze. Later, he described what happened when the tanker was re-boarded:"We were appalled by the spectacle, but we set to work to put out the fires on the deck where the petrol was forcing its way out through the shrapnel holes. All but one of the hoses were burnt, and we had to work with buckets of water from the sea. Chief Pollard, with George Willey, the third engineer, and John Boyle, a greaser, made their way down to the engine room through three feet of water, and got the pumps going, which meant we could use the hose to fight the fires. It took eleven hours before we got them under control. Somehow, the engineers got steam up, and the ship was under way."

The question then was which way they should go? Westward would be safer, but against the wind and weather; eastward lay their destination in the

Clyde, but also the enemy's U-boats and aircraft. There was another brief discussion. "We've come this far with the petrol," was the general opinion. "Let's finish the job." A system of lights was rigged up to pass signals from what was left of the bridge to the engine room, Chief Engineer Pollard wrote on his log: "9th Nov. Resumed passage." Next day, John Boyle died from internal injuries, aggravated by exposure in the lifeboat. The engines were stopped, and his body was committed to the deep.

The next problem was how to navigate the tanker. The wireless, charts and instruments had gone, the compass was showing a massive deviation (the effect of all the broken metal on the ship) and the main steering gear was broken. All 2nd Officer Hawkins had to work with was the sun by day, the stars by night, and a sixpenny atlas. "We ought to make a landfall," said Hawkins,

"somewhere between Narvik and Gibraltar." In fact, he found Clew Bay on the west coast of Ireland eight days after the *San Demetrio* had been reported lost, and she continued her voyage to Rothesay in the Firth of Clyde, where, at the crew's insistence, her own pumps and pipes were used to discharge 3,000,000 gallons of precious gasoline. Captain Waite, meanwhile, and the remaining twenty-two members of the crew had been taken aboard the SS *Gloucester City* and landed at St. Johns, Newfoundland on 12th November.

When Chief Pollard and others were honoured at a lunch in London, he paid a tribute to the *Jervis Bay*'s crew: "While we have such men as those guarding our convoys and waterways, we shall not go hungry." Some of those who heard him added in their hearts: "And with such men as these to sail our tankers, we shall not go short of fuel."

Charles Pollard and George Willey were awarded a very special medal—Lloyd's Medal for bravery at sea. Pollard also received the OBE, and they all shared in the £14,700 salvage money that Eagle Oil paid out to the crew. They wanted "Yank" Preston to have the *San Demetrio*'s tattered Red Ensign, but he could not be found, and the flag remains in the London office of the company to this day.

"British tanker makes a great film story," was the headline in the Sunday Express when the Ealing Studios film "San Demetrio" was shown in January 1944, and the review ended "...the most satisfying fact, which sailors will appreciate, is that the director has avoided every temptation to glamourise the story. For once, it is a report on what happened. It goes into the class of true life dramas...an authentic thriller of the times."

In the early hours of 3rd April 1941, the twenty-two ships of convoy SC26 were in the mid-Atlantic gap, beyond the point at which the Canadian escort had left them, not yet at the point where the escort from the UK was to meet them, and with only an armed merchant cruiser to protect them. Admiral Dönitz could not have picked a better moment for his wolfpack to attack. The *British Viscount*, carrying 10,000 tons of fuel oil, was one of several tankers in the convoy, and William Reuben Virgo Bourner was her 2nd Engineer. What follows is his story of the attack and of its aftermath: "The *British Viscount* was an old steam turbine ship, and we had been having trouble with various auxiliaries, so we had two engineers working six-hour watches. The U-boat attacks started at about 10:30 in the evening of 2nd April, and the first to be sunk was another of our company's tankers, the *British Reliance*. Then a Belgian ship with a cargo of iron ore, was almost abeam of us when it was torpedoed and sank instantly. From then on, ships were sunk at the rate of roughly one an hour.

No increase in speed was ordered until about 3:15 am when, hearing the engine telegraph ringing, I went below to order the men to open the extra nozzles on the turbines. A few moments later, we heard a terrible grinding sound above the noise of the turbines, and the ship heeled over 20 degrees. I shouted to the 3rd Engineer to stop, and ordered the 4th and a fireman to get out, while I opened the astern valve to bring the ship to a stop as soon as possible. The 3rd Engineer and I shut the master valve to the boiler oil pumps as we went aloft. There had been no messages from the bridge during this time, and when we reached the boat deck I could see why: the ship was a mass of flame, and the fire was rapidly spreading aft.

One lifeboat was in the water, and we slid down the ropes and climbed aboard. We had some dificulty in getting the boat's bow round, as the crew had dropped it on the weather side, but that proved to be lucky because, by the time we got it away from the tanker, the oil was burning on the water and it was getting pretty warm. Just as we were pushing off, a cabin boy managed to get out of a port-hole amidships, and we were just in time

You should provide a means to open the potato locker quickly. Get a sack of potatoes in your lifeboat, and a sack of onions, if possible, or turnips. Because of their high water content, these vegetables will serve a double purpose in your rations. Canned tomatoes are important. Do not pass up the bottles of jam. The sugar in them will provide energy. If possible, set your watch to Greenwich time. The mate in your boat may not have a chance to set his watch. He will not be able to calculate longitude with any accuracy without Greenwich time when taking sights. If time permits, get two or three of the rockets which are stowed on the bridge. Be sure your lifeboat is equipped with a flare pistol. Take a roll of toilet paper with you. A Mason jar will keep your matches and other small items dry. Night puts an added burden on you and you must take extra precautions, because at night there is sure to be more panic than in the daytime.
—from *HOW TO ABANDON SHIP* by Phil Richards and John J. Banigan

How
to
Abandon
Ship

Phil Richards • John J. Banigan

CORNELL MARITIME PRESS

to catch him as he floated by. By then, the *British Viscount* was a blazing inferno.

About three hours later, we found one of our firemen on a small raft, and pulled him on board—with some difficulty because the waves were six or seven feet high. That made twenty of us in the lifeboat, out of a crew of 48. We had lost the captain, three deck officers, the radio officer, chief steward, engine room crew, carpenter and sailors. We had a senior apprentice in the boat, who said that the nearest land was Greenland, about 200 miles away, and we decided we would have a better chance of being sighted from a rescue ship if we stayed near the tanker, which by now was just a hulk.

After about twelve hours, a destroyer, HMS *Havoc* [probably *Havelock*, authors], came into view and picked us up. Very good to us they were, too. More survivors were picked up during the next few hours, bringing the total up to seventy. Another destroyer was also in the area, picking up survivors. We heard later that we had lost ten ships that night—nearly half the convoy. At least, the Navy got one of them: two days later, our destroyer made full speed for twenty minutes or so, and came to two corvettes, with a U-boat close by, which turned turtle and sank as we watched. One of the corvettes lowered a boat to pick up the crew."

In September 1941, the 12,842 ton *San Florentino*, another Eagle Oil ship, twenty-two years old, sailing in ballast from the Clyde, quit the convoy after leaving port, and proceeded on her route to Curaçao, off the coast of Venezuela, where she was to load with gasoline. On 27th September, she was sighted through the periscope of *U94*, and shadowed for two days. As night fell on the second day, an epic fight began, which lasted for two hours, the tanker taking evasive action, and returning fire with her 4.7 inch gun. At last, she was hit with torpedoes, first on

Death is only an old door Set in a garden wall. / On gentle hinges it gives at dusk, When the thrushes call.
Along the lintel's green leaves Beyond the light lies still, Very willing and weary feet
Go over that sill. / There is nothing to trouble any heart, Nothing to hurt at all. / Death is only a quiet door / In an old wall.
—*Death is a Door*
by Nancy Byrd Turner

far left: A floating mine displayed at the Maritime Museum of the Atlantic, Halifax, above left: Cdr. E.S. Fogarty Fegen, RN, of the *Jervis Bay*, left: *HMCS Ville de Québec Gets a Sub* by Harold Beament.

Everything turns upon the Battle of the Atlantic, which is proceeding with growing intensity on both sides. Our losses in ships and tonnage are very heavy and, vast as our shipping resources which we control, the losses cannot continue indefinitely without seriously affecting our war effort and our means of subsistence.
—Winston S. Churchill

right: Looking into the engine room of *Empire Unity*, August 1942, below: Cooks at work in the galley of *Empire Unity*, part of a Malta convoy.

the starboard beam and then on the port. With the tanker badly damaged and listing heavily to port, Captain Davis and his crew fought on, and holed the U-boat's conning tower. Then, the tanker was hit again, and a fourth torpedo struck the death blow. She was holed amidships, the whole breadth of the vessel, and began to break in two.

The *San Florentino* went down some 900 miles east of Newfoundland, but her fore part stayed afloat, grotesquely vertical, with the stem protruding a hundred feet into the air. Third Officer Todd and Able Seaman Clayton climbed

up, and sat astride the bow for thirteen hours, until they were rescued by HMCS *Mayflower*. The gun crew, meanwhile, had managed to launch an undamaged lifeboat, but another, the starboard midship boat, was stove in and only just afloat, with its gunwales under water. Sitting waist deep in this and in a bitter wind, nine of the nineteen men aboard died of cold and exposure in the eleven hours that passed before the boat was found. Captain Davis and twelve members of his gallant crew went down with the *San Florentino*.

The next month, October 1941, six tankers were sunk by U-boats and another damaged.

"What you have to remember," said a tanker sailor, "is that she's in ballast half the time, with water in her tanks, and then she's the safest ship afloat". When a tanker was loaded, however, there was very little freeboard, and even a moderate sea would wash across the decks. Another tanker man remembers an Atlantic crossing when a northerly gale and a heavy sea between them swept away the lifeboat and davits on the weather side.

When the *San Vulfrano* was being loaded with aviation spirit for the RAF in Britain, crewman Thomas Rowe overheard a longshoreman say, "If they get hit with that load aboard, the crew won't need life jackets to keep them up—they'll need parachutes to bring them down."

The heat from a burning tanker could be felt at a range of 1,500 yards, and the fire could go on burning for six hours. At other times, a stricken tanker might erupt like a volcano and be gone in the twinkling of an eye. That was what happened to the 8,000 ton *San Victorio* off the coast of Venezuela on 17th May 1942. She was on her maiden voyage, full of aviation petrol from Aruba Island, when she was hit by a torpedo from *U155* and immediately caught fire. Two vast explosions followed. The first blew gunner Anthony Ryan, who was standing on the poop, over the stern rail

and far into the sea. Somehow, this sturdy man kept afloat for sixteen hours, without a lifebelt or any form of raft, in a sea full of shark and barracuda. He was the sole survivor of the *San Victorio*.

All in all, the first eight months of 1942 were a bad time for tankers, especially for those of Eagle Oil, who lost seven, with 269 officers and men, mostly off America's east coast or in the Caribbean Sea. Indeed, they were not good months for anyone in the Merchant Navy or the Merchant Marine. "Milch Cow" submarines, replacing the supply ships, were replenishing the raiders' fuel, provisions and torpedoes, and keeping them at sea for much longer than before. There were more big Type IX U-boats, more reliable torpedoes, and a lot of young Kapitänleutnants, all determined to make their names as aces, now that Günther Prien and Joachim Schepke had gone down and Otto Kretschmer was a prisoner-of-war.

It was the American "industrial miracle" which gave a silver lining to the dark clouds of the year. Although the great advances in ship production had not yet been reflected in the tanker fleet (the sixty-two built in 1942 did not make up for the losses), by the end of May 1943, production had been stepped up to fourteen or fifteen a month and, for the first time, U-boat sinkings were exceeded by new ships. The T-2, which was typical, was 523.5 feet long, had a beam of 68 feet, a draft when loaded of nearly 30 feet, turbo-electric power, a speed of 14.5 knots and a dead weight of 16,165 tons. The T-3 was a little bigger, with a dead weight of 18,302 tons, and a speed of 18 knots.

There was, however, no respite for the tankers in the early months of 1943. Convoy TM1 sailed from Trinidad for North Africa on 28th December 1942, with nine tankers carrying fuel oil and other military stores. Operation Torch had been a brilliant success, but now the Allied armies and air forces were trying to drive Rommel's Africa Corps out of Tunisia and bring the campaign to an end. They needed fuel for their tanks, trucks, aircraft

You have seen him on the street rolling round on groggy feet, / You have seen him clutch a lamp post for support. / You have seen him arm in arm with a maid of doubtful charm / Who was leading Johnny safely back to port.

You have shuddered in disgust as he sometimes bites the dust, / You've ignored him when you've seen him on a spree. / But you've never seen the rip of his dark and lonely ship Ploughing furrows through a sub-infested sea.

You have cheered our naval lads in their stately iron-clads, / You have spared a cheer for infantrymen too. / You have shuddered in a funk when you read 'big mail boat sunk', / Did you ever give a thought about the crew? .

Yet he brings the wounded home through a mine-infested zone / And he ferries all the troops across at night. / He belongs to no brigade, he's neglected, underpaid, / But he's always in the thickest of the fight.

And he fights the lurking Hun with his ancient 4 inch gun / And he'll ruin Adolph Hitler's little plan. He's a hero, he's a nut, he's the bloody limit—but He's just another Merchant Navy man.
—anonymous

All ships' officers (engineers and mates) had their own cabins which, on tankers, were quite good. The baths had no running, fresh water so baths had to be taken in a bucket! The firemen and greaser's accomodation was not very good as it was in the forecastle with most of them in one berth. A good, small library was supplied by the Flying Angel seaman's mission.
—William R.V. Bourner, engineer

above: William R.V.Bourner

and coastal craft, and TM1's tankers were bringing 25 million gallons of it. The convoy was accompanied by a Royal Navy escort group consisting of the destroyer HMS *Havelock* and three Flower Class corvettes. There would be air cover from America for the first day.

The convoy formed two columns, two ships in each, with the ninth ship sailing on the starboard wing. Six hours out from Trinidad, a report came from a patrolling Catalina of a U-boat sighting some few miles ahead. *Godetia*, one of the corvettes, hurried to the reported spot and, more in hope than anger, dropped a pattern of depth-charges. The next three days were peaceful, but the convoy had been sighted from *U514*, en route back to base from the Caribbean. The convoy's course, speed and position were radioed to Lorient, and Admiral Dönitz ordered six U-boats,

lying between Madeira and the Azores, to sail south at their best speed and intercept. *U514*, meanwhile, was instructed to shadow the convoy, but Kapitänleutnant Auffermann did more than that. In the early evening, he torpedoed *British Vigilance*, leading the centre column, and her voyage ended in one vast explosion.

In the wheel-house of the *Empire Lytton*, immediately astern, Captain Andrews turned hard to starboard to avoid the burning hulk. Then, in silhouette against the flames, he saw the U-boat lying on the surface, and an avenging instinct made him swing the wheel again to ram. Smoothly, *U514* slid away beneath his bows, but not before a young apprentice, leaping to an Oerlikon, had scored hits on the conning tower with an accurate burst of 20 millimetre shells. When the tanker *Narvik* joined in with a few rounds from her 4 inch guns, Auffermann submerged, but continued following the convoy. Two hours later, the *Empire Lytton* caught up with the convoy and took the *British Vigilance*'s station in the lead. But now the escort ships were running low on fuel, and when an attempt was made to refuel from the *Narvik*, which carried the necessary pipe-lines, the seas were too rough to carry out the transfer. The escort commander ordered a northward change of course for calmer water, and that could not have suited the waiting U-boats better. *U381* sighted the convoy, some 600 miles to the west of the Canaries, in the afternoon of 8th January 1943.

The escort ships were having further problems: HMS *Havelock*'s HFDF was operating intermittently, and two of the corvettes had unserviceable radars. When the wolfpack attacked in the evening, the *British Oltenia II* was sunk and the Norwegian *Albert E. Ellsworth* was set on fire. The assault continued throughout the night, and the *Minister Wedel* and the *Narvik* were both hit by torpedoes, but did not catch fire. The escort struggled to protect the remaining tankers. In the early morning hours of 9th January, two torpedoes from *U-442* hit the *Empire Lytton* on the starboard bow, and Captain Andrews knew that his ship could become a furnace within minutes, as the *British Vigilance* had done. There was no fire. The stem was holed, however, and the ship was making water. Andrews decided his best course was to abandon her, and lie off in the lifeboats until dawn. The decks, davits and falls were smothered with thick, black oil from the ruptured forward fuel tanks, and the launching in the darkness turned into a nightmare. One boat was never found, most men took a soaking, and the Chief Officer was drowned.

When Andrews re-boarded the tanker in the morning of 9th January, with 31 survivors from his crew of 47, he was at once faced with an order

from the escort commander: if the *Empire Lytton* could not get under way and make 8 knots, she must be abandoned and would be sunk by gunfire. As the Chief Engineer could promise nothing better than 6 knots, she was abandoned once again. From the bridge of the corvette HMS *Saxifrage*, Andrews saw a flash and a column of black smoke on the horizon and, saddened, turned away. *Havelock*'s guns, however, had not sunk her: five hours later, she was still afloat when Korvettenkapitän Hesse, returning in *U44*, fired his last torpedo into her.

Meanwhile, the stricken *Narvik* and *Minister Wedel* had gone down, and the *Albert L. Ellsworth* had been finished off by *U436*. By nightfall on 9th January, only three of TM1's tankers were afloat, and the wolfpack had not finished yet. In the evening of 10th January, four U-boats slipped between the escorts on the surface and launched their attacks. The *British Dominion* was hit, and blew up with her load of avgas. Only the *Vanja* and the *Cliona*, watched over by a Catalina and with three more warships in their escort, reached North Africa—the sole survivors of convoy TM1.

After the Allied armies had gone ashore in Normandy, and were advancing into France, they, too, needed vast quantities of fuel to keep them on the move. The preparation for Pluto (pipeline under the ocean) had long been in hand and, in July 1944, a pipeline was laid from the Isle of Wight to Cherbourg. Before Pluto came on stream, a fleet of tankers, known as the Hamble Circus, carried fuel from the Solent to the invasion beaches and later to the liberated Channel ports. When the big motor tanker *Empire Russell* carried a million gallons into Cherbourg on 27th June, she was the first Allied merchant ship to enter a north European port for more than four years.

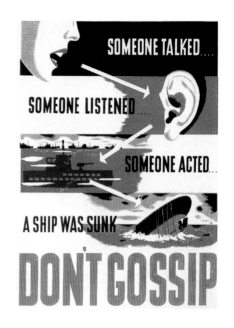

above left: The comfortable cabin of the Chief Officer on board a tanker in 1941.

The freedom of the seas is the *sine qua non* of peace, equality and co-operation.
—from an address to the United States Senate, January 22, 1917 by President Woodrow Wilson

A modern fleet of ships does not so much make use of the sea as exploit a highway.
—from *The Mirror of the Sea* by Joseph Conrad

ACCORDING TO THE MYTHS of ancient Rome, Jupiter, as ruler of the universe, decided to allot certain parts of planet earth to his brothers, and he assigned the sea to Neptune (or Poseidon, as the Greeks would have it). From that time on, Neptune tended to eschew Olympus in favour of his new domain, and to make his home within its depths. It was believed that he could call up the wildest storms, or quell them, according to his whim—a facility of which the poet Homer was to write:
"He spake, and round about him called the clouds
And roused the ocean—wielding in his hand
The trident—summoned all the hurricanes
Of all the winds, and covered the earth and sky
At once with mists, while from above the night
Fell suddenly."

One Merchant Navy skipper put it less poetically: "You can't beat the sea, it's stronger than you are." The proof was always there. Without any form of assistance from the enemy's mines or bombs, guns or torpedoes, King Neptune contrived that approximately 1,000 Allied ships, should be lost in the course of World War II.

There were sometimes twelve convoys at a time crossing the Atlantic, with over 20,000 men engaged. They might be under escort by warships or, when they were in what was known as "the mid-Atlantic gap" or "the graveyard", they might not. Always, they were restricted to moving at the speed of the slowest ship among them. For Able Seaman Thomas Rowe, who served on merchant ships throughout the war, "the North Atlantic was the worst ocean I ever travelled, with ferocious storms and mountainous waves, the power and weight of which was really terrifying, especially at night when you could only see the fluorescence on the crests as they reared up alongside the ship. Nearing the coast of America or Canada you usually ran into fog, which added to the hazards of sailing in convoy. It was not uncommon to be fogbound for two or three days in that area."

# ROLLERS

There is nothing more enticing, disenchanting and enslaving, than the life of the sea.
—from *Lord Jim* by Joseph Conrad

The sea hates a coward.
—from *Mourning Becomes Electra*, by Eugene O'Neill

It is difficult to row in a heavy sea. The men can last at it about fifteen minutes, and by making every stroke count, can perhaps get a half mile from the ship. Be sure you do not start pulling on the oar before it is in the water. Keep your eye on the stroke oar on each side of the boat. Put the weight of your body on the oar. In a boat properly rowed a thrumming noise issues from the oars and gives a sense of timing.
—from *HOW TO ABANDON SHIP* by Phil Richards and John J. Banigan

There were fifty-three days in the last three months of 1941 when the winds measured force 11 on the Beaufort scale, i.e. up to 75 miles per hour. Many ships lost their places in the convoy, lost touch with the Convoy Commodore, and suffered heavy weather damage which caused long delays in port while they were repaired. The one redeeming feature was that the U-boats' activities were also severely restricted by the weather, and few merchant ships were lost in November and December of that year.

For people who spend their lives close to a coastline, the sound of the sea can be serene and soothing, even soporific, as it gently stirs the pebbles on the foreshore and slaps against the rocks; at other times, when an incoming tide is allied with high winds, the sea can show a more ferocious aspect of its nature. Then, it can rear, pour over the promenades, and lash against the piers. But it is not until a man goes aboard a ship and ventures far from land, that he begins to realise what a raging monster the sea can sometimes be, towering and cascading, with a noise like nothing else on earth.

Some will thrill to the experience, to the sound, sight and feel of it; some will be awestruck, even terrified; others will simply suffer *mal de mer*, and devoutly wish they were not there. The ordinary merchant sailor, and his comrade in the Navy, will just accept it as a normal part of life.

In July 1941, a group of survivors had been adrift for eighteen days, and their small supply of water had run out. A Lascar deck-hand lay in the bottom of the lifeboat, clearly dying of thirst. Seated beside him, an engineer decided that nothing could be lost by attempting an experiment. He stirred a little of his precious toothpaste into a mug half-full of sea-water, raised the Lascar's head and persuaded him to drink. After an hour, the Lascar opened his eyes, sat up, and in due course recovered sufficiently to take his turn at paddling the boat. Later, the toothpaste manufacturers

Ports are necessities, like postage stamps or soap, but they seldom seem to care what impressions they make.
—from *Arrival At Santos*
by Elizabeth Bishop

How holy people look when they are sea-sick!
—from *Notebooks*
by Samuel Butler

There is nothing more enticing, disenchanting, and enslaving than the life at sea.
—from *Lord Jim*
by Joseph Conrad

Roll on, thou deep and dark blue Ocean—roll! Ten thousand fleets sweep over thee in vain; / Man marks the earth with ruin—his control Stops with the shore.
—from *Childe Harold's Pilgrimage*
by Lord Byron

overleaf: *Passing?* by Harold Beament, right: January 1944, the Canadian frigate HMCS *Swansea* riding out rough seas.

were asked if their product contained an ingredient which might make sea-water potable. The reply was: "Not so far as our chemists are aware".

The way to be popular on board a lifeboat, if and when the emergency arose, was to try to remember, before you left the ship, to snatch up something that might stand you and your shipmates in good stead: a packet of biscuits, a tin of sardines, first aid dressings, and as many bottles of beer as you could find. Any man with a mouth-organ could be sure of being persona grata on the boat. That was in the early days, and by the autumn of 1942, it had become clear that the equipment in many merchantmen's lifeboats was inadequate to meet the demands of an escalating war. Men had survived the sinking of their ships, only to die slowly of cold, thirst, starvation or exposure in a hopelessly ill-equipped craft. Investigations showed that certain ship owners had not even seen fit to meet the most basic of requirements for the safety of their crews. The rules were then officially examined and enforced, and they included the replacement of the bulky, standard life-jackets by buoyant, yellow waistcoats with battery-operated red lights (an idea inspired by the equipment used by London bus conductors for inspecting tickets in the blackout), and the provision of brightly-coloured, weather-proof suits.

Other equipment to be carried in lifeboats included water-pumps (to obviate baling), apparatus for distilling sea-water, fishing lines, concentrated food in tablet form, lamps which lit automatically on contact with the water, smoke signals and rockets, folding ladders, side-screens and canopies, rain-catchers, needles and twine, whistles, signalling mirrors, oil for massaging, compasses and charts. Rations were increased and water stocks were trebled. "They're putting so much stuff in now," was the laconic reaction of

I considered the North Atlantic ocean the worst ocean I have travelled, with ferocious storms and mountainous waves crashing aboard. The power and weight of these waves were really terrifying, especially at night in pitch darkness when you could only see the fluorescence on the wave crests as they reared up alongside the ship. As you neared the coast of America or Canada, you usually ran into thick fog which also added to the hazards of sailing in convoys. Two or three days of being fogbound was not uncommon in this area.
—Thomas Rowe, Ordinary Seaman

The dragon-green, the
luminous, the dark, the
serpent-haunted sea.
—from *The Gates of
Damascus, West Gate*
by James Elroy Flecker

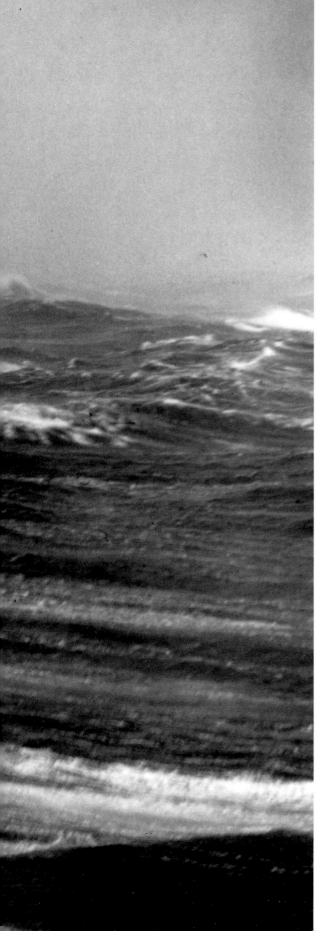

left: A merchant ship in a British convoy to Russia, rides out heavy weather in February 1945, below: Hoisting an oil hose in a refuelling effort, a sketch by Felix Topolski.

Water, water, every where,
And all the boards did
shrink; / Water, water
every where, / Nor any
drop to drink.
—from *The Ancient
Mariner*
by Samuel Taylor
Coleridge

We went southwards
through the minefields and
then into the English
Channel where we saw
overhead great flights of
cargo gliders being towed
over to the continent by
planes for what we found
out later was the start of
the Normandy Invasion.
Our first call back in
Canada was at Halifax
where we anchored in the
very deep water of Bedford
Basin to discharge our
ballast. I found this
operation very interesting
as they dropped a little
bulldozer into each hold
and it pushed our pit shale
ballast into piles that a
crane grab could bite into.
The grab rushed up out of
the hold and just flung its
load into the harbour
which was amply deep
enough to swallow all that
we had carried over the
ocean.
—Robert Atkinson,

right: Robert Atkinson,
engineer, far right:
R.S. Snell, steward.

the hardened seaman, "that there's no room for
us." Lifeboats had skates fitted to their bottoms,
so they would slide down the side of a listing ship,
and rafts were made reversible, in case (as often
happened) they went into the water upside-down.
Further regulations required that every ocean-
going ship's crew should include three radio
officers, and that at least one of her lifeboats
should be powered by a motor, with sufficient fuel
for 160 miles. Tanker crews were issued with
flame-resistant overalls and hoods.

Seventeen hands from a ship that was torpedoed
a few degrees north of the Equator in the South
Atlantic survived in some style for twelve days on a
raft. Their provisions included biscuits, corned
beef and condensed milk, and to these the young
Commander of the U-boat which had sunk them
added cigarettes, chocolate and a bottle of cognac,
before bidding them farewell. In the course of
their voyage, two men contrived to seize a turtle
by its fins and to hoist it aboard. After due
consideration, however, they decided to return
the startled creature to the deeps. Later, having
fashioned hook and line, and with flying fish for
bait, they caught themselves a shark, which they
boiled with salt water in a chocolate tin. The meat,
so cooked, was white and firm, and pronounced
entirely edible. When picked up by a Spanish
freighter, all the survivors were in fair condition,

apart from sunburn and salt water blisters.

The weather took no sides in the Atlantic battle,
it was fair or foul to all according to its mood. The
U-boat crews could escape the worst of it while
they stayed at depth but, once they surfaced, they
were liable to suffer more than most. Herbert
Werner, described how it was in January 1943,
when *U230* joined a wolfpack in the North
Atlantic. "Water that poured in through the open
hatch and sloshed around our feet, and the high
humidity within the hull caused food to rot, the
skin to turn flabby, and our charts to dissolve. The
smell was brutal. The extra fuel we carried in our
bilges sent out a penetrating stench; our clothes
reeked of it and our food took on the taste of oil
and grease...The sea boiled and foamed and
leaped continually under the lash of gales that
chased one another across the Atlantic from west
to east. *U230* struggled through gurgling
whirlpools, up and down mountainous seas; she
was pitched into the air by one towering wave,
caught by another and buried under tons of water
by yet another. The cruel winds whipped across
the wild surface at speeds of up to 150 miles per
hour, whistling in highest treble and snarling in
the lowest bass."

The years of World War II produced unique
spectacles which anyone who saw them will
always remember. No-one can forget the sight of
the night sky above a city under air attack, lit by
searchlights and twinkling bursts of flak, of a
battleship, heavy with armament, setting out from
port, of a division of USAAF heavy bombers
heading east in combat formation from an
assembly point somewhere in East Anglia. Another
unforgettable sight, was of a major convoy,
steadily advancing with ensigns fluttering,
creamy bow waves, spreading washes, the long,
low tankers in the centre columns, fast-moving
destroyers and sloops patrolling the flanks, and a
great, grey cruiser or a carrier in their midst—all
set against an awesome, ever-changing seascape.

K136

THE TRAMP STEAMER of the 1930s, now almost extinct, was basically a vessel with a box-shaped hull and a sparse superstructure, always built for maximum capacity, and low-powered for economic operation. Normally a tramp displaced less than ten thousand tons and steamed at about ten knots. Many were launched at shipyards in the north-east of Britain, where there was a long tradition of ship-building. A tramp could be away from home for perhaps two years, sailing no fixed routes, and always available to the highest bidder for carrying cheap and easily-handled bulk commodities from and to any port at any time. Crew accomodation in a tramp was of a basic sort. Typical were those which plied from Wales, carrying coal, and returning with timber, ore and grain. A liner, on the other hand, was a cargo ship, with a normal displacement of between ten and fifteen thousand tons, and two or three decks to facilitate loading and stowage. She could also carry passengers, and would run to a schedule on an advertised route between fixed places, at a speed some five knots faster than a tramp.

The crew of a liner normally wore uniform, the crew of a tramp did not. If such a thing would be suggested, a tramp sailor's reaction would probably have been: "What, wear fancy dress for going to sea? Not likely, mate."

Big items of cargo, such as locomotives, Sherman tanks and two-engined bombers, often had to be carried on the decks, because the hatches were not big enough to lower them into holds.

In 1940, and for some years after, the armament on most merchant ships consisted of 4 inch and 12 pounder guns that dated from World War I, and there were certain difficulties in mounting them on board. The merchantmen were not designed to carry weaponry, and sight-lines were obstructed by rigging, derricks, and other fixtures. There was also the problem, when guns were being mounted, of allowing for the top weight and balance of the ship. The armament was originally

# TRAMP

NAVY DEPARTMENT
WASHINGTON
CONFIDENTIAL
30 MARCH 1942
FROM: THE SECRETARY OF
THE NAVY
TO: ALL SHIPS

1. It is the policy of the United States government that no U.S. Flag merchant ship be permitted to fall into the hands of the enemy.
2. The ship shall be defended by her armament, by maneuver, and by every available means as long as possible. When, in the judgement of the Master, capture is inevitable, he shall scuttle the ship. Provision shall be made to open sea valves, and to flood holds and compartments adjacent to machinery spaces, start numerous fires and employ additional measures available to ensure certain scuttling of the vessel.
3. In case the Master is relieved of command of his ship, he shall transfer this letter to his successor, and obtain a receipt for it.
—Frank Knox

left: *On Escort Duty*
by Harold Beament

below: A coal-loading facility in Halifax during the war, right: Taking cargo aboard the *Jussi H* in Halifax.

manned by the Merchant Navy men themselves, after a three-day course in gunnery with the Royal Navy; later, trained gunners of the DEMS (Defensive Equipment Merchant Ships) took over, and by 1944 they numbered 35,000, including 13,000 soldiers of the Marine Regiment of Artillery. They were serving on 7,000 ships, from the biggest liners to the smallest tugs. Commanded by a Petty Officer or senior NCO, the DEMS then formed the nucleus of a ship's gun crew and

trained other seamen to support them. Their counterparts in the American Merchant Marine were the Naval Guard, led by an Ensign (the equivalent of a Royal Navy Midshipman) who, because of his short, intensive training, was sometimes referred to as a "ninety-day wonder".

To keep a tramp on station in a convoy was a formidable task. If she fell astern, or wandered off her course, she could seldom make the speed to regain her place. That might put the Commodore

In Liverpool alone, 30,000 dock workers handled more than 75,000,000 tons of cargo during the war. More than 4,500,000 troops moved through the port of Liverpool between 1939-45.

in something of a quandary: should he slow the convoy down, order a dog-leg for a while, to let the straggler catch up, or leave her to her fate? The chances were that he had told the masters at his conference before the convoy sailed "I will not leave you alone," and he would stay true to that.

Tramp steamers formed the bulk of the vessels on the Russian convoys, and in the Arctic winter, from mid-December until late in May, they needed ice-breakers to make a way for them. Furthermore, they had to maintain a position close astern of the breaker, or the ice would have reformed.

The tramp seamen bore almost half of the casualties sustained by the Merchant Navy during World War II—most of them in the Atlantic battle.

On 11th January 1940, Jack Armstong from Hull nervously climbed a rope ladder from a lighter to the deck of the SS *Dalesmoor*, a Walter Runciman line tramp which was lying at anchor in Liverpool Bay. His fibre suitcase, containing two white jackets and a suit of dungarees, all provided by the owners, plus his worldly possessions, was hoisted up after him. He was seventeen years old and small for his age, timid and bespectacled, and he had never been to sea. Nevertheless, the engineer's mess boy had failed to present himself, and Jack was his replacement. He found himself in charge of a tiny pantry and a mess room big enough for three of *Dalesmoor*'s engineers at any one time. His supply of water had to be fetched from below in the engine-room, and he soon learned to hurry up a few rungs of the ladders as the ship's bows fell in the water, and to hold on hard as she rose and the force of gravity tried to tear the bucket from his hand.

"The catering staff," said Armstrong, "consisted of the Chief Steward, who also served the Captain, and an assistant who looked after the navigation officers, me, and the cook, who fed the crew of thirty-five. There was no refrigerator, only a cold

After a short leave, the Merchant Navy Pool instructed me to travel to Scotland where I boarded the *Queen Mary* for passage to New York. There I spent three or four weeks in the St George hotel in Brooklyn whilst waiting for the *Empire Battleaxe* to be built. We were treated exceptionally well in New York. All the USO clubs, women's voluntary organisations, etc had something to offer...coffee and doughnuts, dancing and one or two women's organisations gave us a shoe box parcel filled with all manner of useful items...hand-knitted pullovers, socks, Balaclavas. We were also given free tickets to cinemas and theatres. I was given a job to relieve the boredom of waiting for the ship to be finished. I worked as a busboy at Stouffer's restaurant in Grand Central Station. I was paid 30 dollars a week plus tips.
—Charles Bishop, steward/cook

far left: A North Sea convoy of 24 ships, above: Tommy Howard and Charles Bishop, 1942.

**convoy** a protective escort. The word entered the English language as long ago as the fourteenth century, coming from the Latin *conviare*, to travel with, via the Old French *conveier* or *convoier*, to accompany. However, it acquired the specific connotation of protection only during the sixteenth century. During World War I, beginning with the sinking of the passenger liner *Lusitania* in 1915, German submarine attacks on Allied shipping became an ever-increasing hazard, so that Allied troop and supply ships were obliged to travel in convoys protected by destroyers. The same practice continued during World War II. Both as a noun and as a verb, convoy retains the military sense of protection against the enemy, but it also is used in civilian affairs, as, for example, a motorcycle convoying a visiting dignitary.
—from *Fighting Words* by Christine Ammer

right: *Night in Dockland, September 1940*, by Felix Topolski, on the next spread: *Rescue Tug Approaching a Steamship* by Norman Wilkinson.

store, where the food slowly deteriorated as the ice melted. Then we were reduced to salted meat or corned beef. Like most old ships, the *Dalesmoor* was alive with cockroaches, which fell from the steam pipes into the stew-pans on the cooking range, while the weevils and maggots got into the flour from which the cook made bread. You could pick them out, but there were times when you were so hungry that you didn't bother any more. All the food was severely rationed, and the Runciman line were well known for its 'starvation boats', as were many other tramp lines. The old seamen knew them all. The Captain and the Chief Steward were responsible for victualling the ship, and everybody knew that they paid the chandlers first-class prices for third-class provisions, and shared the difference between them."

Armstrong's first voyage with the *Dalesmoor*, in May 1940, was west-bound to Canada. "Convoys didn't always have an escort in those days," he said, "and we took a zig-zag course, but our main protection from the enemy was the weather, which in winter was severe. It was a fearsome sight to see a huge wave towering over you, then crashing down on the ship and right over the bridge. It was surprising how quickly you learned to walk with your legs apart and to roll with the ship, so you could walk the deck without hanging onto the rails—like walking up and down hills and sideways as well. Sometimes, the seas put the galley fires out, and then we would be down to hard tack—ship's biscuits, that you had to tap on the table to knock the weevils out."

"With the ship in ballast, the screw came out of the water when the bows went down, and the whole ship shuddered. The engineers worked hard, putting on the revs when the screw was in the water, and cutting the power when it was out. There were days when we hardly moved because of that, just bobbing like a cork. It took us a month to do a fortnight's voyage, and we

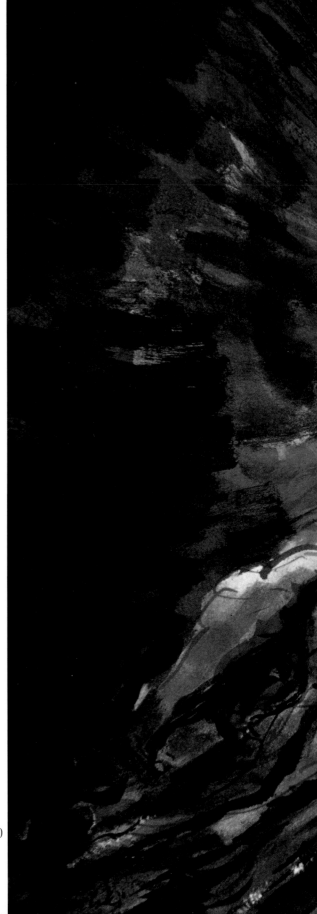

completely lost the convoy. All the engine room activity meant that two engineers had to be there all the time, and they were exhausted. Even the Chief had to turn to, and he was about seventy with poor eyesight, like me. The voyage took so long that the food ran out and we were back on hard tack."

"Taking early morning tea to the 2nd Engineer was rather scary. He never woke up to a vocal call, and if I shook him he came out of his bunk fighting. I think it was from dealing with him that I learned to fear the war. We loaded with grain at St. John in Newfoundland, where the ladies were very good to the crew, providing us with 'comforts' they had hand-knitted—Balaclavas, scarves, mittens, gloves and sea-boot stockings. We assembled at Halifax with a convoy of twelve ships, again without an escort, and we were soon attacked by a U-boat. There was a tremendous explosion, and I dashed on deck to see the ship next to us in the column with its stern sticking up. She was loaded with ore and sank quickly, and there was a second explosion with a great gush of steam and water as the boilers blew up. The order was given to scatter, which was our method of defence then, and as we moved away, increasing speed, there were two more explosions."

"We made our own way after that, eventually joining up with two other ships before we were met by two corvettes two days out from England. There were all kinds of craft in the Thames, and it was only then that we learned about Dunkirk. No radios were allowed on board, and the ship's radio was only switched on at certain times for distress messages, incoming orders and the like, so we had no news of what was going on in the war, either at sea or on the land. We didn't know about the heavy bombing raids, and when I went home to Hull, I was appalled at the damage. The city was virtually dead, and my family had moved to Huddersfield."

The Sea is Woman, the Sea is Wonder— / Her other name is Fate!
—from *Virgilia*
by Edwin Markham

Implacable I, the implacable Sea; Implacable most when most I smile serene— Pleased, not appeased, by myriad wrecks in me.
—from *John Marr and Other Sailors*
by Herman Melville

The sea speaks a language polite people never repeat. It is a colossal scavenger slang and has no respect.
—from *Complete Poems*
by Carl Sandburg

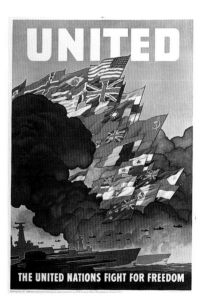

left: French Admiral
Aboyneau (left)
aboard a Free French
corvette heading for
St.Pierre, above:
Jack Hawkins in a
scene from the film
*The Cruel Sea.*

125

HMS *Begonia* was refitting in the Royal Albert Docks, London, preparatory to being handed over to the U.S. Navy. The American crew arrived, but with no officer. The difference to British crews was startling. "Say Cap, where's the coffee, we don't drink tea." "Say Cap, we sure been on board a whole week and no chicken yet. When we gonna have chicken?" "Say Cap, there's no Coke on board. When you gonna get the Coke?" "Say Cap, there's no freezer on board. How we gonna get ice cream?" ...and so on. After four weeks the American officers arrived and I attended the commissioning ceremony. The White Ensign was hauled down and the Stars and Stripes was hoisted. She became USS *Impulse*. HMS *Calendula* was also refitting at the same time and became the USS *Ready*. Together the two corvettes crossed the Atlantic and their respective captains reported their arrival to the US Admiral in Argentia. They marched before the Admiral, saluted, and one said, "Sir, I have the *Impulse*". The other said, "Sir, I'm *Ready*." The Admiral took a long look at them and replied, "And what the hell d'you expect me to do about that?"
—A.H. Pierce, (C.O.) HMS *Begonia, Godetia, Spiraea*

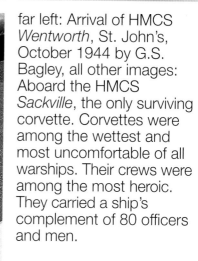

far left: Arrival of HMCS *Wentworth*, St. John's, October 1944 by G.S. Bagley, all other images: Aboard the HMCS *Sackville*, the only surviving corvette. Corvettes were among the wettest and most uncomfortable of all warships. Their crews were among the most heroic. They carried a ship's complement of 80 officers and men.

right: General De Gaulle decorates a corvette officer, below: HMS *Godetia, K226,* commanded by Lt.A.H. Pierce, RNR, centre: Officers dining in the wardroom of a Free French corvette, bottom centre: HMCS *Barrie* in the North Atlantic in 1941.

left: Capitaine de Frigate Bisot on board FFS *Alysse*, and senior officer of the French Flotilla of corvettes operating from the Clyde naval base, below: A still from the film *Corvette K225*.

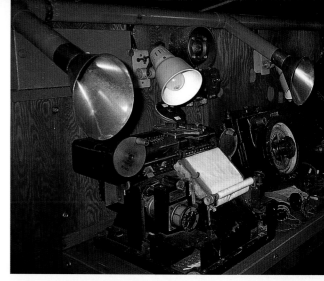

far left: Cyril Hatton, Leading Telegraphist, HMS *Snowflake*, left: Asdic Hut, HMCS *Drumheller* by T.C. Wood, all other images: Scenes of HMCS *Sackville* now moored at Halifax, Nova Scotia.

left: Survivors of a torpedoed merchant ship crowd the deck of their rescuer, the corvette *Arvida*, in her arrival at St. John's in August 1942. below: Robert Seager, L/SA, HMCS *Timmins*, K223.

below (both): Jack Belcher, HMS *Wallflower*, K44, right: *Convoy Afternoon* by Donald C. Mackay

Hail *Clematis*! Thou wert not born in lady's bower / Thou'rt sterner stuff, though still the Flower of Chivalry. / To keep the freedom of the seas for those / Who take their business to the sea in ships— Protecting, succouring and befriending them through all: A very Flower of Chivalry!

Hail *Clematis*! Born in a city of the West / Where "ship-shape, Bristol fashion" was our boast of old / And still is!—Go forth to conquer evil things / To slay, exterminate and crush beyond uprise / All that is wrong and holding souls of men in bond. / We hail thee *Clematis*! The Flower of Chivalry.
—from the ship's builders, Charles Hill of Bristol

# RUN TO THE RED STAR

OF ALL THE ROUTES sailed by the Allied merchant fleets in World War II, the north-east route to Russia will surely be remembered as the one which posed the greatest challenge to the seaworthiness of ships and the hardihood of men. There were other routes as hazardous, and others as arduous, but none which combined the dangers with the hardships like the Russian run. It was a route on which the merchant ships and their escorts were under threat of attack by the enemy all the way from the hour of their departure until the hour of their return. From their bases on the north Norwegian coast, the Luftwaffe commanded much of the route with Ju-87B "Stuka" dive-bombers, He-111 torpedo bombers, Ju-88 light bombers and the four-engined reconnaisance Focke-Wulf Condors. Packs of U-boats, some withdrawn from the Atlantic, patrolled the Barents and Norwegian Seas; and at any time, one of the German big ships might emerge from the fiord where she lurked— the 43,000 ton battleship *Admiral von Tirpitz* with her formidable armament, the cruiser *Admiral Hipper*, and the fast pocket battleships *Admiral Scheer* and *Lützow*, all with their attendant escorts of destroyers.

For seamen who were unaccustomed to the nature of the Arctic, there was the striking contrast between seasons: the perpetual daylight hours of summer and the ferocious weather and long nights of winter, when dawn and twilight were divided by an hour and when an unseen "growler", drifting from the icepack, could tear a hole in a ship below the water-line. "In the ice," said one Convoy Commodore, "it's better to be loaded than light. When you're light, the rudder and propellers may strike ice and be damaged; loaded, they're below it, and they're safe."

The winter scene was spectacular: the forecastles, bridges, hoists, davits, lifeboats and deck cargoes thick with milk-white ice, the sea-spray freezing where it struck. There was beauty, also, on the Arctic journey with the eerie, multi-coloured splendour of Aurora Borealis, shimmering and flashing in the polar sky.

In the early summer of 1941, Hitler decided that his duplicitous non-aggression pact with Stalin had run its course, and that the time had come to put their relations on a more realistic footing. He launched Operation Barbarossa on 22nd June, and over 160 German divisions, strongly supported by the Luftwaffe, attacked on a 500 mile front. The British Empire and the Union of Soviet Socialist Republics were allies from that moment on. No matter that Stalin had taken cynical advantage of the British and French preoccupation with the western front to sieze the eastern part of Poland and annex the Baltic States, no matter that Russia had supplied Germany with oil and grain up to the very eve of Barbarossa—all that was in the past. Hitler had contrived by a single cataclysmic act to bring about an alliance, uneasy as it might sometimes prove to be, between Moscow and London, between the philosophically incompatible forces of Marxism and capitalism.

In his subsequent history of the war, Winston Churchill told a tale, possibly apocryphal, about a Royal Marine who, at that time, was being shown the sights of Moscow by a Russian guide. "This is the Eden Hotel," said the guide, "formerly the Ribbentrop Hotel. And here is Churchill Street, formerly Hitler Street, and this is Beaverbrook Station, formerly Göring Station. Will you have a cigarette, comrade?" The Marine accepted. "Thank you, comrade, formerly bastard."

The outcome was that, in the Anglo-Soviet Trade Agreement of August 1941, Britain granted Russia a five year credit of £10,000,000 at 3.5% interest, and the first convoy of military aid sailed from Loch Ewe in Scotland, assembled at Hvalfiordur, an inlet on the west coast of Iceland, which had been occupied by the British and Canadians in May 1940 to pre-empt an invasion by the

Though displaying elan and gallantry, neither the Soviet navy nor its air force ever relieved the Home Fleet of any appreciable share of the responsibility for the defence of an Arctic convoy.
—from *The War at Sea*, by S. Roskill

The Soviet Government had the impression that they were conferring a great favour on us by fighting in their own country for their own lives. The more they fought the heavier our debt became.
—Winston S. Churchill

Through icy, fog-bound seas, their flanks exposed to the dive-bombers, surface raiders, and submarines moving out from the Nazi-held fiords of Norway the slow gray convoys moved—and kept moving. Nor was there sanctuary at their destination, for every hour on the hour, it was said, the black-crossed planes of the Luftwaffe blasted heart-breaking delays in the grim business of unloading the ships in the ice-cluttered harbor of Murmansk. Yet the cargoes were delivered.
—from the post-war report by the American War Shipping Administration to President Harry S. Truman

The design for the Victory ship was completed in 1943 and the first ship was delivered in 1944. The Victory was turbine-powered with 8,500 horse power and she cruised at 15 knots. 414 of the Victory ships had been built by the end of the war, and an additional 117 were built after the war, some of which saw service in the Vietnam war.

Be sure your lifeboat is seaworthy. This may seem needless advice. Yet in the past bottoms have come out of many lifeboats. One lifeboat of a United Nations freighter, torpedoed 200 miles from Bermuda, leaked so badly that for eleven days the men were unable to stop baling.

Every man should have a whistle made fast around his neck, so that if he is in the water, he can blow the whistle to draw attention. Life lights are manufactured for both jackets and life rings. With good visibility these lights will provide a possibility of attracting rescuers within a radius of at least four miles. Within the visibility range of shore, they offer a three-way chance of drawing attention—from land, sea, and air.

If you are on watch, you should have your life suit, extra clothes, and abandon-ship package with you, so you will not have to lose time returning to your quarters. Do not take it for granted that all the equipment required by law is in your lifeboat. Norman Lee Sampson, the third assistant of a torpedoed freighter, reported that

right: *Routed North* by John Hamilton

Germans. Hvalfiordur means "fiord of the whale", but was more often thought of by all who passed that way as "that God-forsaken place". On 21st August 1941, the first convoy sailed from Britain for Archangel on the River Dvina (which was ice-free in the summer months). It comprised six elderly tramps carrying wool, tin and rubber, with fifteen Hurricane fighters packed into their holds, and was escorted by three destroyers, three mine-sweepers (well-armed vessels, and as fast as a corvette), and three anti-submarine trawlers. Interference by German surface ships was discouraged by a Home Fleet cover force as far as Bear Island, and the convoy was closely followed by the veteran aircraft carrier HMS *Argus*, with a strong RAF contingent and twenty-four Hurricanes, which later flew off her flight deck and landed safely on the Russian airfield at Vaenga in the Kola Inlet.

The first convoy was code-named Operation Dervish, while subsequent outbound convoys were coded PQ (after the initials of Commander Peter Quellyn Russell, and Admiralty planner), and homebound convoys were logically QP. In January 1942, when the effect of the Japanese air assault on Pearl Harbor was to bring Britain a truer and more welcome ally, President Roosevelt and Prime Minister Churchill, meeting in Washington, agreed that they must first defeat Germany before turning on Japan, and that, as a corollary, they must at all costs "keep the Russians in the war". It meant that America would join Britain in providing Marshal Stalin's forces with a growing volume of military supplies.

Originally, the Anglo-Soviet Agreement had been signed on the basis that the supplies would be loaded onto Russian freighters at British and later at American ports, but few such ships materialised, and it transpired that the Soviet Union neither had, nor ever would have, enough to undertake the task. The whole burden of the Russian convoys was to fall on the hard-pressed

below: Loading in Halifax prior to convoy assembly in Bedford Basin.

British Board of Admiralty and, in particular, on Admiral "Jack" Tovey, C. in C. Home Fleet. He knew that the escorts had to come from the resources of Western Approaches Command, where they were manifestly needed. He did not like that, nor did he care for the committment, least of all in summer, and he said so, but Churchill was the boss, and the job had to be done.

Beginning in July, a monthly quota of at least 400 tanks and 300 combat aircraft were allocated to the Russians, and the convoys went on sailing, every ten or fourteen days, until the war was won. Towards the end, it entailed the assignment of warships to merchantmen on a ratio of one to one, but the convoys still went on. The total cost of the equipment carried to Russia by ships registered in Britain was £428,000,000.

When the merchant seamen stepped ashore in Murmansk, the conditions that they met were, as was to be expected, exceptionally bleak—the enemy, after all, was only thirty miles away. Almost every building on the miles of waterfront had been damaged or destroyed by Luftwaffe bombers. The citizens seldom showed much sign of friendliness and, with a shortage of cranes, transportation and skilled labour, unloading cargoes took an age, while a queue of ships lay at anchor in Vaenga Bay, waiting for their turn. Ironically, the port, whose name in the local language meant "the end of the earth", had been built with British aid in 1915 at the behest of the Tsar.

On 20th March 1942, convoy PQ13, made up of nineteen ships, British, American, Panamanian and Polish, assembled off Iceland and set course for Murmansk. Covering the first stage of the convoy's passage, and hoping to lure the German big ships out of the Norwegian fiords into battle, were two British battleships, a carrier, three cruisers and eleven destroyers, while the convoy's close escort consisted of the cruiser HMS *Trinidad*, in which the escort commander, Rear-Admiral Bonham-

nine of his shipmates were trapped in a lifeboat with no oars. The boat drifted into a sea of blazing oil.
—from *HOW TO ABANDON SHIP* by Phil Richards and John J. Banigan

It started with a single aircraft, possibly an old friend, a four-engined Focke-Wulf reconnaissance plane which closed the convoy from eastwards and then began to go round them in slow circles, well out of range of any gun-fire they could put up. It had happened to them before, and there was little doubt of what the plane was doing—pin-pointing the convoy, shadowing it, noting exactly its course and speed, and then reporting back to some central authority, as well as tipping off any U-boats that might be nearby. The change this time lay in the fact that it was occurring so early in their voyage, and that, as they watched the plane circling and realized its mission, the sun was pouring down from a matchless sky on to a sea as smooth and as lovely as old glass, hardly disturbed at all by the company of ships that crossed it on their way southwards. Unfair to peace-loving convoys, they thought as they closed their ranks and trained their glasses on the slowly-

circling messenger of prey: leave us alone on this painted ocean, let us slip by, no one will know....
—from *THE CRUEL SEA* by Nicholas Monsarrat


After much messing about we arrived at a quay in Archangel where we were to load timber. This went on for days being entirely done by women. Each afternoon about 4 pm the local school mistress brought her 14 and 15 year-olds down to the quay and these girls loaded timber til 8 pm. Our food stocks had long run out, and two consignments of stores had been sent for us on PQ17 but both had been lost so we were living on black bread, ship's biscuits and odd bits of reindeer. We even went ashore and collected large quantities of blueberries— of which there was a limited supply— and made jam, as we did have some sugar. Lifeboat biscuits appear to be made of a striated rock. The secret is to soak them overnight in a bucket of water, get the oven literally red hot, and insert the soaked biscuit. The instantaneous generation of steam causes the biscuit to rise like a Yorkshire pudding and the puffy mass covered with sweet blueberry jam is quite palatable.
On 24th August we had our first air raid in

Carter, flew his flag, two destroyers, and three ex-Norwegian whalers earmarked as reinforcements for the Russian Navy's mine-sweeper fleet. Convoy QP9, meanwhile, also well-escorted, was half-way along its homeward route.

The two-way operation had been carefully planned, but few plans survive their first contact with the enemy, particularly in Arctic weather. Convoy QP9 ran into a severe storm on 24th March, but managed to keep formation and continue west, while PQ13 had a harder time of it. In a strong south-westerly gale, mountainous seas and heavy snow, station-keeping was almost impossible, as was communication with the Convoy Commodore in the *River Afton*. The look-outs were blinded and numbed by the cold, and the convoy had become, not an integrated unit, but a collection of individual ships proceeding approximately east. Furthermore, whenever there was a break in the cloud cover, Ju-88s based at Banak and Petsamo took the opportunity to make a series of attacks. On HMS *Trinidad*, Captain Sanders broke radio silence (and his orders) to acquaint the Admiralty, Admiral Tovey and the Senior British Naval Officer North Russia with the deteriorating situation.

On 27th March, when PQ13 should have made a rendezvous south of Bear Island, only seven vessels were in the vicinity, and *Trinidad*, with a destroyer, set about the task of rounding up the rest. The *River Afton*, meanwhile, had been isolated and, having evaded the attack of a surfaced U-boat, all the Commodore could do was to continue on the way to Murmansk on his own (sadly, the *River Afton*, which had first sailed on the Russian run from Iceland with PQ1 on 28th September 1941, did not survive the later horrors of PQ17).

That night, the *Induna* was endeavouring to tow the armed trawler HMS *Silja*, which was almost out of fuel, through the ice, when she was torpedoed. Her lifeboats were crowded, and injured men lay freezing while the remainder tried

to bale. In one boat, fourteen men died in the next three days, and their bodies were dropped overboard, before a Soviet mine-sweeper arrived to save sixteen survivors. Of the ten men alive in the other lifeboats, two died later in a Murmansk hospital.

Three German destroyers of the Eighth Flotilla, *Z24*, *Z25*, and *Z26*, now sailed out from Kirkenes, between North Cape and Murmansk, to intercept the convoy, and soon found the survivors of the 7,000 ton *Empire Ranger*, which had been sunk by bombing, freezing in their lifeboats. Another lifeboat, containing thirty-eight men, had floated for six days in appalling weather before being sighted from a Russian tug. Only the bosun and a fourteen-year-old cabin boy, both badly frost-bitten, had survived, and the bosun's legs and arms had to be amputated to save the poor man's life.

*Trinidad*, still hunting up the remaining stragglers, sighted the destroyer *Z26*, and there followed an inconclusive exchange of shots. It was *Trinidad*'s bad luck that the special low-temperature oil in her torpedo tubes had frozen, and when that was cleared and a torpedo was launched, it had a gyro malfunction. Turning back whence it came, the rogue torpedo blew a hole in the cruiser's port side, rupturing an oil tank and flooding the forward boiler room. The enemy destroyers, however, now turned back to the south-west, hotly pursued by the destroyers *Fury* and *Eclipse*, which caught *Z26* and sank her with gunfire. *Trinidad* eventually reached the Kola Inlet with Russian tugs in close attendance, but not required to give assistance. Five merchant ships, totalling 30,000 tons, had been lost from the complement of PQ13. Once ashore in Murmansk, the survivors were subjected to heavy air attack every day and night for the next three weeks.

HMS *Edinburgh*, now Bonham-Carter's flagship, was lying off Vaenga in the Kola Inlet on 27th April 1942, preparing to escort QP11 on the homeward route, when a lighter came alongside from which,

# GIVE US THE SHIPS

ALEX COLVILLE '41

## WE'LL *finish* THE SUBS!

Archangel, mostly an incendiary raid in darkness. Fortunately, there was little wind so damage was limited. Time went on and our food supply became ever more desperate. We seemed to be cursed with the worst cook it has ever been my lot to sail with. When he had food he spoiled it so that lots was thrown away. We just had to eat what we could get. The sailors and firemen went on strike until the food, particularly the bread, improved. Lack of yeast was the problem, as no attempt had been made to grow fresh yeast before our existing stock was exhausted. Eventually we obtained some black bread from ashore...not much to our liking, but better than nothing. Jam making from blueberries continued and it was much appreciated as it was the only pleasant confection we had.
—H.G. Hall, engineer

left: A fine example of World War II poster art for the cause of the war effort, by D.A. Colville.

I was 17 years old. There was no mess boy and I was a hasty replacement. The pantry was just big enough for a sink against the bulkhead and a set of cupboards to form a work bench athwartships. The mess room was equally small and there was barely room for four people, but whilst at sea, there were only three in in at any one time. There was no water supply to the sink, and I had to take a bucket down to the engine room whenever I wanted water for whatever purpose. This meant travelling up and down perpendicular ladders. I soon learnt the art of running up a few steps with a full bucket when the ship was dropping in the water, reducing the gravity on the bucket, and then hanging on like grim death when the ship rose again whilst the bucket became as heavy as lead. The sink was provided with a steam pipe so, after half filling the sink with water (no more because of the movement of the ship), I turned on the steam to heat the water. This made a terrible noise as the steam pipe expands and the steam bubbles in the water. This meant I could not heat the water during the engineer's meals and the dishes were often washed in cold, greasy water. The water was heated and used many

under the eyes of Soviet soldiers and Royal Marines, a number of heavy boxes were loaded on board. It was not ammunition, however, which went below into the cruiser's magazine, but five tons of bullion for the United States Treasury—payment for American war supplies.

The thirteen-ship convoy sailed the next day, and was soon sighted by a pack of U-boats. The attacks began on the 30th, and *Edinburgh*, steaming ahead of the merchant ships, was hit by two torpedoes which destroyed her stern, her rudder and her two inner screws. She could be of no help to the convoy in that condition, and with four destroyers and two mine-sweepers for protection, Captain Faulkner turned back to Murmansk, while QP11, brilliantly defended by the remaining two destroyers and four corvettes, continued westward through the ice.

Next day, *Edinburgh* was well down by the stern, her list was steeper and she could not be steered. More U-boat attacks were beaten off, and a tow was attempted by HMS *Foresight*, but when three German destroyers appeared, Bonham-Carter ordered the line to be cast off. By now, the cruiser was swinging round in circles, but she and her destroyers continued to maintain a fierce rate of fire. Then, she was hit twice more by torpedoes, and the Rear-Admiral told Faulkner to give the order to abandon. Two mine-sweepers, HMS *Harrier* and *Gossamer*, came alongside to take off her crew, and Bonham-Carter hoisted his flag in *Harrier*. As he and Faulkner gazed at the slowly settling cruiser, the Captain had a sudden thought. In quieter moments, he and the Rear-Admiral had amused themselves by playing backgammon, and Faulkner was the better player. "I'm going back on board her for a moment," he said. "What the devil for?" asked Bonham-Carter. "For the tally," said Faulkner, "you owe me thirty pounds!" The other shook his head: "I'm afraid the tally goes down with the ship, and with the

Russian gold."

Bonham-Carter arrived in Murmansk to find HMS *Trinidad*, with her plates patch-welded, braced with lengths of rail-track "borrowed" from the Russians by a naval raiding party, but with only her after boiler room capable of providing steam for the turbines. Nevertheless, his flag was hoisted and *Trinidad* set out from Murmansk with four destroyers to catch up with QP11. In the Barents Sea, the merchantmen and warships came under heavy air attack and, on 15th May, a Ju-88 hit *Trinidad* with a cluster of four bombs. Down by the bow, and listing to starboard, the cruiser fought on, and her gunners had the savage satisfaction of destroying her attacker, but her fuel tanks were ablaze, the fire was spreading, and Captain Davies was obliged to give the order to abandon ship. An Engineer Lieutenant insisted on going below to ensure that all of the stokers had emerged, and he did not return. His award of the Albert Medal was posthumous. HMS *Foresight* manoeuvred carefully alongside to take off her surviving crew and passengers—the injured seamen of PQ13—and the HMS *Matchless* administered the *coup de grâce* with a couple of torpedoes.

Since Bonham-Carter sailed with PQ14 as escort commander, five warships had gone down under him, of which *Trinidad* was the last. A well-liked officer, if unlucky at backgammon and in his choice of flagships, it was he who was perceptively to write: "We in the navy are paid to do this sort of job, but it is beginning to ask too much of the men in the Merchant Navy. We may be able to avoid bombs and torpedoes with our speed. A six or eight knot ship has not this advantage."

On 16th June 1942, one of PQ13's survivors, the *Empire Starlight*, sank in the shallow water of the Kola Inlet. Almost every day, from 4th April, when she anchored off Murmansk, until she was finally unloaded and abandoned, the German bombers seemed to seek her out for particular attention. Her master, Captain Stein, could have been forgiven for believing that the Luftwaffe was pursuing a personal vendetta against him and his Chinese crew. After persistent and almost daily bombings in mid-April, during which her gunners accounted for three of her attackers, she was only kept afloat by the heroic efforts of Russian divers and her crew. The bombing was relentlessly pursued throughout the month of May, when she was loaded with pit-props and timber for the journey back to England, and if she was not the most bombed vessel in the merchant fleet, she must have run the record-holder very close. The award of OBEs to her Captain and Chief Engineer cannot be regarded as being over-generous, but it is good to know that, after the war, the *Empire Starlight* was raised, refitted, and resumed her trade.

The Soviet Admiral Golovko, commanding Russia's Northern Fleet, came to enjoy a love-hate relationship with the Royal Navy, and indeed the US Navy, whose members, and especially the officers, he tended to regard as capitalist imperialists—the sort of men who would have been on the Tsar's side in the revolution of 1917. This view was shared by many Soviet officials. Golovko deplored the way a British naval escort would sink a stricken merchant ship with gunfire, having taken off her crew, rather than risk her cargo falling to the enemy. He took the view that such action should only be taken when it was absolutely certain that salvage was impossible.

Meanwhile, the Red Army had counter-attacked with enormous courage, and there had been appalling losses on both sides. "We have seriously underestimated the Russians," confided General Heinz Guderian, pioneer and main protagonist of German tank warfare. There was a stalemate for a while until, in the summer of 1942, Hitler took personal command, and soon his armies in Russia

were moving east again, killing and capturing thousands of prisoners. Marshal Timoshenko's Army Group was forced back to the River Don, and ordered to defend Stalingrad to the last man. It is ironic that, at a time when Stalin was urging the Allies to "open a second front in Europe", battalions of Red Army POWs were, albeit unwillingly, helping the German Todt construction gangs to strengthen the Atlantic Wall of the Führer's Fortress Europe.

Gradually, the Russian port facilities improved, due largely to the efforts of Royal Navy working parties, joined by US Navy men. Often under air attack, they worked under the direction of the Senior British Naval Officer North Russia, a Rear-Admiral, whose tasks included obtaining assistance for the convoys from Russian destroyers, mine-sweepers and ice-breakers, of organising anchorage and berthing for the merchantmen, and of their replenishment with fuel, water, stores and ammunition for the homeward run. These tasks were never easy, and they also embraced the even more demanding one of liaison with the hard-nosed Admiral Golovko. For the majority of visitors, contact with the Russians was largely through interpreters, many of whom were women, few of whom were helpful, and most of whom were either members of, or closely connected with, Russia's secret police force, the NKVD.

Relations between the Royal and Merchant Navies were always rather tenuous, and the tensions of the Arctic convoys almost brought them to the breaking point. Rightly or wrongly, by mid-summer 1942, some merchant seamen were beginning to suspect that, as well as helping "Uncle Joe", there was another reason for the Russian run, and that was to tempt the German big ships out onto the high seas, where they might come within the range of the British Home Fleet's guns. "Their Lordships in London don't give a toss for us," was the general tenor of this feeling, "nor for the

times before it became so filthy it just had to be replaced.
—Jack Armstrong, Steward

Rudy Radmanovich was a member of the U.S. Merchant Marine in World War II. In the winter of 1944 he shipped out of New York as an oiler aboard the Liberty ship, SS *Stephen Leacock*. The ship was routed to Halifax where they picked up an escort for the north of England. In the Hebrides they joined another convoy which set course north through the Norwegian Sea, the Arctic Sea and finally, the White Sea north of Archangel. In navigating the North Cape, the convoy was caught between Nazi planes, submarines, mines and surface warships. They went as close to the ice pack as they could, but were unable to evade the German attacks. 14 of the 34 merchant ships of Rudy's convoy managed to reach Russia. 20 of the vessels were sunk in the ice-choked waters, and few of the crew members survived. Rudy served on in the Merchant Marine throught the end of the war. He was awarded the Merchant Marine Combat Bar, the Atlantic, Mediterranean and Pacific War Zone medals, the Merchant Marine Victory medal, as well as the Russian Medal of

Russkis either, come to that."

Rear-Admiral Hamilton, the commander of PQ17's cruiser escort wrote in his operation order: "The primary object is to get PQ17 to Russia, but an object only slightly subsidiary is to provide an opportunity for the enemy's heavy ships to be brought to action". It was, after all, inherent in a navy man that he should regard the sinking of the *Tirpitz*, or of any German battleship, as a more important matter, in the wider context of the war at sea, than the protection of freighters taking arms to Russia. So the seamen's suspicions may not have been entirely without foundation.

Among the supplies reaching Russia by the northern route (and these were in addition to the greater quantities which came through the Persian Gulf and thence by rail from Basra to the Caspian), were 7,400 aircraft, including 3,000 from America, 5,200 tanks (1,390 from Canada), 5,000 anti-tank and anti-aircraft guns, 4,000 rifles and machine-guns, 1,800 radar sets, 4,000 radios, 2,000 sets of telephone equipment, 14 mine-sweepers, 9 motor torpedo boats and 4 submarines. There can be little doubt that this materiel, plus ammunition and torpedoes, medical supplies and hospital equipment, food and industrial plant, tin, wool and rubber, were of crucial help to Marshal Stalin's armies. These supplies enabled the Russians to withstand the German invasion, eventually to repel it, to win the great tank battle on the plains of Kursk in 1943, and to move onto the offensive to such good effect that they not only drove the Wehrmacht back, but continued moving west until they reached the German capital before the Western Allies.

Between August 1941 and May 1945, forty convoys, each comprising roughly twenty merchant ships, made the voyage to Russia; ten per cent of the ships involved were sunk by the enemy en route, while act of God or accident accounted for the loss of nineteen more. The ships which carried the equipment from America, and

Commemoration for the Murmansk Convoy Survivors.

The *Schoharie* was berthed only a few streets from the Navy Yard and when we reboarded, her winches and booms were rolling cables in and out as cargo was hoisted aboard from the dock and lowered into the hatches for storage. Pallets of jerry cans filled with gasoline and crates of heavy duty ammo were being stored below. "Goddamnm we're not a tanker", Lagola, the coxs'un yelled. Nevertheless, the loading of the jerry cans and the ammunition continued on for several days until finally the hatches were closed and secured with tarpaulin. Next came the deck cargo: locomotives, trucks, and huge wooden crates. The whole deck and hatches fore and aft, were packed solid with deck cargo. We wondered whether the ship would sail or sink under such a load. And the locomotives were stenciled in white paint with lettering the that didn't make sense: 0006095ARKHSU775698. Of course, this was the manufacturer's code or perhaps, the shipping agent's. We figured it out later. The next evening a dozen cartons were delivered to the Navy crew and upon opening them, found foul weather gear and athletic and game equipment. The Armed Guard was well-equipped for the expected bitter cold of the Atlantic. We were issued cold weather, sea arctics, winter trousers (lined bibbed overalls), winter mittens, winter face masks and goggles and heavy parka jackets, in addition to the standard sou'wester rain hat, oilskin coat and trousers. There surely was no secret where we were headed and many guessed we were going to Murmansk, Russia. The scuttlebutt gang were always speculating on every rumor and hunch that occurred to them. And so the guessing game began. But for the time being the only important thing was a last night of liberty. "Button your lip!" and "Loose lips sink ships" the signs read as we departed the ship. Fortunately, having a last night at home for the locals, and a good time in New York for the rest, probably did more to keep those lips closed. A few may have used "We're shipping out soon" to gain an extra kiss or more from a worried young lady. We don't know that anyone used the guessing game of our destination, except, perhaps, "It's gonna be damn cold wherever we're

those which took it on to Russia, sailed under many different flags, and from 1942 onwards the US Navy often assisted in escorting them. The responsibility, however, of mounting the convoys, and seeing them through the 2,000 miles or more from Iceland, at longitude 20 degrees west, to Murmansk or Archangel, at 33 or 42 degrees east, fell to the Royal Navy.

The threat from the enemy—surface warships, U-boats or aircraft—had to be accepted by every man who sailed the seas in wartime, and the brutal cold and ever-present ice that made the Russian run a peculiarly horrible experience. It was small comfort to the Allied seamen to know, as they crept between North Cape and Bear Island, and through the Barents Sea, trying to maintain some sort of formation, that conditions in the Arctic Circle were as hostile to the Kriegsmarine as to the navies of the Allies.

Few merchant seamen particularly enjoyed the time they had to spend on Russian soil, where they often found suspicion, waste and ingratitude. To move about in town was to run the gauntlet of unfriendly guards at every gate and doorway, who could be relied on to find some discrepancy in any pass or ID papers. Mail was interferred with or delayed, and any Soviet official, whether male or female, who showed signs of a friendly disposition, would soon mysteriously disappear. It angered the seamen to see lines of new Hurricanes, which had been brought to Russia at great risk, standing idle and uncovered, open to the elements, because the Russians were too lazy, or too inefficient, to repair some minor damage caused on landing or unloading.

The survivors of that most ill-used of convoys, PQ17, in their time ashore in Archangel, subsisted on a diet of black bread, barley and grass soup, and, with the local medical resources overwhelmed by the battle casualties from the front line barely thirty miles away, the treatment

for their injured was primitive at best. "There was only one redeeming feature," said a stoker, "the vodka was cheap."

Not all the defects, however, were on the Russian side. The charge was laid at Murmansk (and seized upon by Stalin), that cargoes loaded in Britain, as opposed to in America, were often found to have been damaged en route, arguably due to the British method of putting the heaviest items low in a ship which, the Russians claimed, tended to make the vessel laterally unstable and, as she rolled, to cause the lashing wires to penetrate the packaging and lacerate the goods.

There were a number of occasions when the heavy units of the opposing navies sailed in all their pomp across great stretches of the northern seas, the one under orders to destroy a convoy but, on no account, to get into a battle, the other directed to engage the enemy if possible but, on the other hand, to protect the convoy. Signals flashed through the ether from London and Berlin: Ultra decryptions were suggesting one thing, while B-dienst intercepts indicated another, and the big ships altered course accordingly. Consequently, it was only the aircrew, flying off the carriers or launched from the battleships, who got to fire a shot in anger.

The voyage of convoy PQ17 in June 1942, was a disaster. Most of the escort was withdrawn by the Admiralty in London to meet what turned out to be a non-existent threat from the *Tirpitz*, leaving the merchantmen to struggle on to Archangel, virtually undefended. It was also, unhappily, the first combined Anglo-American naval operation. Of the thirty-five merchant ships which set out from Iceland, eight were sunk by aircraft, and eight by U-boats, which also finished off another eight already damaged by the aircraft. This slaughter was achieved at a cost

previous spread: *Barrington Street Patrol, Halifax* by Thomas Charles Wood, below: In February 1945, a Liberty ship on the homeward journey from Russia rides out a storm as part of a heavily defended British convoy, on following spread: Survivors of a sinking merchant ship are brought aboard a Canadian rescue vessel during the Battle of the Atlantic.

going". But then it was late September and at sea cold weather comes early. The mystery letters we later realized were Arkangel, Soviet Union, a rather obvious message to anyone who cared to know.

—Thom Hendrickson, DEMS Signalman, U.S.N.


I don't know how we ever slept on the Russian run. We had no heating whatever down below, other than a coal-burning stove on the messdeck, which we could only use when the chimney could be erected, sticking up on the foredeck, if the weather permitted. The condensation from our breath built up into ice six inches thick inside the messdecks as, of course, the deck above had no wood, only bare steel. We spent the whole time wrapped up in anything we could find. At sea I was supposed to sleep in the wheelhouse outside the wireless office, so as to be on immediate call. I wore a one-piece Kapok zipped up suit which had an oilskin outer cover for working on the upper deck. I had also obtained a pair of wooden-soled fisherman's boots in Iceland, which were very efficient and, over my shoulders, as I could not wear it any other way, a duffle coat. The night

to the enemy of six bomber aircraft. 153 merchant seamen and one Royal Navy man were killed, and it was probably those figures which, more than any other, gave rise to the feelings of resentment on the one side and of shame upon the other. The feelings within the Merchant Navy led to condemnation and recriminations, stated or unstated, which have cast a long, dark shadow down the years. When at last the survivors arrived in Glasgow with the inbound QP14, they were addressed by the Ministry of War Transport's Under-Secretary of State, who found it in himself to say of their ordeal that "whatever the cost, it was worth it", before he was shouted down.

Meanwhile, a Soviet Navy Captain on Golovko's staff had declaimed at a post-convoy conference: "It is not enough, we want more tanks, more planes..." Marshal Stalin would have approved of that. In due course, four of the merchant Masters were awarded the Distinguished Service Order, the first of their service to be so decorated. More significantly, in the context of the war, the Arctic convoys were suspended for the next two months of constant daylight, and when PQ18 sailed from Loch Ewe on 2nd September 1942, it was with a Home Fleet cover force, its own light carrier carrying three Swordfish and six Sea Hurricanes of the Fleet Air Arm, and two destroyer squadrons—one for close escort and one to range freely, giving battle wherever it was offered. Despite this high level of support, thirteen of the forty-eight ship convoy were sunk, ten by torpedo-bombers, but the gallant, steadfast conduct of the Royal Navy escort did much to restore the respect of the American Merchant Marine, if not entirely of the British Merchant Navy.

During those two months, when only half-a-dozen comparatively fast single ships made the Russian run, Admiral Tovey did his best to provide succeeding convoys, both PQ and QP,

with strong, fighting escorts, adequately supported by fleet oilers, through the most dangerous sectors of their routes. The additional destroyers could only come from the Western Approaches Command but, as Dönitz was withdrawing U-boats from his Bay of Biscay bases to patrol the Barents Sea, a sort of balance was maintained in the Atlantic. Despite continuous attacks throughout the war, the German bombers had few successes against the merchantmen in the Kola Inlet, and the reason may have been the prodigious, if sometimes ill-directed, anti-aircraft barrage thrown up by the Russians and from the ships themselves. In addition to the *Empire Starlight*, as has been recorded, only three merchantmen were sunk, while another two succumbed to mines in Murmansk Roads.

One survivor of PQ18 was a 1st Mate, who reached the south island of Novaya Zemlya, alone in an open boat, and scrambled ashore to replenish his supply of fresh water. Glancing at the rocks below, he observed a flock of ducks and, with more hope than confidence, let down a length of rope with a running bowline on the end. One of the birds promptly inserted its head, and he continued angling until he had collected enough to live on roast duck (the resourceful fellow contrived to light a fire) for the remainder of his stay on the island.

The saga of the Russian convoys took a better turn in the autumn of 1944, when 159 ships made the voyage and not a one was lost. Overall, however, the Royal Navy had lost 18 warships and almost 2,000 officers and men, while 87 merchant ships had gone down with an average of a hundred men on each. For their part, the Germans had lost a battleship, three destroyers, thirty-two U-boats and as many aircraft. It had been a bitter and prolonged battle. With its surviving veterans, it rankles that the Merchant Navy's heroic contribution was never recognised by a campaign medal.

It was when he was presenting Russian

decorations to British officers and seamen who had made many voyages to Archangel or Murmansk, that Mr. Ivan Maisky, the Soviet Ambassador to Britain, spoke of their missions in these terms: "They are a northern saga of heroism, bravery and endurance, and the price had to be paid. This saga will live for ever, not only in the hearts of your people, but also in the hearts of the Soviet People, who rightly see in it one of the most striking expressions of collaboration between the Allied Nations."

before our return some of us were invited to attend a cinema show on board *Edinburgh* and the Russian sentries posted on every gangway annoyed us with their insistence on seeing our identity cards every time we passed them. Of course, at that time we knew nothing of the millions in gold bars being loaded on the *Edinburgh* and soon to spend many years at the bottom of the Barents Sea. Our original escort group sailed on 28th April again with the two Russian destroyers escorting QP11 and very quickly ice started to form again all over the ship, the upper deck crew keeping themselves warm by chipping off ice from the guns and depth charge throwers. Within two days the *Edinburgh* had been torpedoed by *U456*, but did not sink. However, she could only go around in circles with the ship largely out of action. At this time six German destroyers moved in to finish off the *Edinburgh* and our destroyers *Amazon, Bulldog, Forester* and *Foresight* took them on in a classic line gun battle, helped by *Edinburgh*'s guns. The leading German destroyer, the *Hermann Schoeman*, was blown out of the water, which discouraged the others, but by 1st May, *Edinburgh* had sunk with all the gold.
—Cyril Hatton, Leading Tele-graphist, HMS *Snowflake*

below: The Jack Currie crew. Currie is second from the left.

OF ALL THE AID provided by America to Britain in the early years of World War II, not the least important was the training of pilots. This piece of the Lend-Lease package stemmed from an offer by General Henry "Hap" Arnold, Commander of the US Army Air Corps (as it then was), to the RAF of a third of the places in his expanding training programme. It was a generous offer, which was gratefully accepted, and between June 1941 and February 1943 over 7,500 embryo RAF pilots crossed the Atlantic to take their places in the "Arnold Scheme", as it was called. Nearly 4,500 young hopefuls completed the training successfully and returned to Britain with their wings. Jack Currie was one of them .

"There were seven of us who had contrived to stay together through the vicissitudes of initial ground school at Stratford-on-Avon and air experience at Ansty, and we were still together on Monday, 5th January 1942, aboard the troopship *Wolfe* as she lay off Gourock in the Firth of Clyde.

The Stratford group's accommodation was not the most salubrious to be found aboard the ship: it was on the mess deck, next to the galley, way back astern and just above the Plimsoll line. A cheerful seaman showed us how to sling our hammocks and, as cheerfully, charged half-a-crown for the two bits of wood which held the ends apart. The resulting contraption didn't look comfortable, but it was—once you had mastered the knack of getting into it without doing a barrel roll. That night, I slept like a baby, while the ship stood silent on the softly lapping tide.

Next day at noon, the *Wolfe* moved out into the Firth and steamed slowly south between the Isle of Arran and the Ayrshire coast. Featonby, one of our number, appeared at the deck rail. "In the canteen," he said, "there's as many cigarettes and chocolates as you want. It's just like peacetime." The coastline faded, the breeze began to penetrate our greatcoats, and we went below to play pontoon until the call for "lights out". Fully

dressed, and wearing a life-jacket (ship's orders were insistent about that), I slept well again. It seemed like a moment before the clatter of cutlery and the smell of bacon frying announced another day, and it took no longer to swing out of the hammock and take a place at table.

To breakfast so, unshaven and unwashed, seemed decidedly raffish, if not downright degenerate—I would not have got away with it at home—but so limited were *Wolfe*'s facilities that anyone attempting their ablutions at that hour of the day did so at the risk of missing breakfast altogether. Featonby, predictably, contrived to rise early, and was as neat as a pin. For the rest of us, two or three days without a razor didn't make much difference to our chins.

When the morning lifeboat drill was held, the ship was steaming southward in the Irish Sea; she passed St. David's Head in the early afternoon and came to anchor in Milford Haven, among the mastheads that protruded through the surface of the sound. "It's a ship's graveyard," said Lawton with a shudder. "I hope we don't stay here long."

"They've been sunk on purpose, mate," said Burt. "Block-ships, they are, to prevent the U-boats sneaking in." He glanced westward down the sound. "The convoy'll form up here, I reckon. Last port of call before the old Atlantic. Safety in numbers, mate, against the U-boats—and the bloody *Tirpitz*."

We stared at this new, nautically knowledgeable Burt. "*Tirpitz*?"

"Your Jerry pocket battleship—don't you know anything about the war at sea?"

"Actually," said Featonby, "the *Tirpitz* is bottled up in the Baltic, and daren't come out."

"Don't you believe it, Ron. It might bust out at any minute and come belting across the Atlantic, looking for such as us. That's why we'll sail in a great convoy, see?"

This forecast of a great marshalling of British sea-power to our side proved optimistic. When the

*Clematis,* a Flower Class corvette built by Charles Hill of Bristol, sailed down the Avon in the late summer of 1940 under the command of a fine seaman and distinguished R.N.R. Commander, York Mcleod Cleeves. She soon knew the hazards of the Atlantic. On her second convoy 37 out of 52 ships were lost. She had towed a merchant ship—the SS *Ardoni*—back to Bristol waters and survived being the sitting target they both were. It was a good example of her Captain's seamanship qualities. It also earned salvage money for the ship's company. Shortly before Christmas 1940 she was one of the escorts of WS5A, a large troop convoy bound for South Africa. In addition to three other corvettes there were three cruisers—*Bonaventure, Dunedin and Berwick*—as well as the aircraft carriers *Furious* and *Argus* loaded with aircraft for Africa. It was a considerable target. On Christmas day *Clematis* was on the starboard bow of the convoy with a merchant ship—the *Empire Trooper*—which had which had strayed off her correct station in the convoy. At 0725 the officer of the watch and the yeoman of signals saw flashes on their starboard bow. They thought it was lightning until, to their alarm, shells started to drop round them. They then saw what they described as a large battleship some four miles off. The alarm bells were rung. The Captain immediately ordered full steam, altered course towards the enemy and ordered the guns crew to open fire. At the same time he ordered a signal to be sent to the Admiralty which he realised would be picked up by the other Naval ships in the convoy: 'Am engaging unknown enemy battleship' and gave our position. It was in fact the *Hipper*, but at that time was thought to be the

right: A Royal Air Force Lancaster bomber, the type flown by Jack Currie, at its dispersal during World War II.

convoy formed, even Burt had to admit that a solitary frigate and another tatty troopship fell short of what he had in mind. Nevertheless, it was in this company that the *Wolfe* set course that afternoon. Next morning, she was in the North Atlantic and rolling on the greenies like an empty barrel. Johnson had been one of those affected by the motion of the tender as it crossed the gentle Clyde; now, he was quite brought down, and sat throughout the day, with others equally distressed, swathed in blankets on the windswept afterdeck, his long, comedian's face a greenish, yellow shade. Mustering for lifeboat drill, we called a hearty greeting, to which he responded with the sickliest of grins.

That afternoon, in what had been the first-class dining room before the *Wolfe* became a troopship, as many of the draft as could be crowded in were treated to a talk by a famous fighter pilot who, on a rest from operations, was bound for a lecture tour in the USA. Squadron Leader Gwilliam was physically slight, with fair, wavy hair a little longer than the norm and a youthful appearance, except for the network of lines around his eyes. He wore his tunic with the top button unfastened, in the fighter pilot's fashion, a row of medal ribbons and a pair of tennis shoes, for which he apologised—he had left a burning Spitfire just too late to save his toes. His talk, from what I heard of it (he spoke very quietly), was about the way the US Army Air Corps trained their pilots. Many of us would have liked to have heard a word about his combat experience but, such were the inhibitions of the day, the obligatory reticence which made the slightest hint of "line-shooting" utterly taboo, that no-one asked the hero to say a word about himself.

In the afternoon of 10th January, Burt announced that a gale was blowing up. The *Wolfe* must have heard him, because she started behaving more eccentrically, adding pitching and tossing to the

154

*Admiral Sheer.* Miraculously, *Clematis* was not hit. The engine room were ordered to make smoke to shield the convoy while *Clematis* continued to close the enemy and continued to fire her 4-inch gun. Fortunately for *Clematis* and her ship's company, the cruisers, and particularly *Berwick*, had by then picked up the signal and had come round from the port side of the convoy. *Berwick* in particular opened fire and, although no match for the *Hipper*, persuaded her to withdraw. As history in German records now shows, *Hipper* did not wish to become involved in a battle early in her cruise. *Clematis* survived and so did *Empire Trooper* in spite of being hit. *Berwick* also suffered damage and casualties. But *Clematis*—a mercifully small target—was unharmed. She survived many more adventures but none so remarkable as that Christmas morning. In his report on Naval affairs to the Commons, A.V. Alexander, the First Lord of the Admiralty, mentioned the action, adding that the signal by *Clematis* 'brought tears to his eyes'. The feelings of the crew as their ship closed the *Hipper* can well be imagined.
—Sir John Palmer,
HMS *Clematis*

rolling and yawing we had come to know if not to love. The path through the water was that of a corkscrew, and the group of the unwell on the after-deck swelled by the minute. Withers, wearing a balaclava helmet that made his head look like a turnip in a badly-holed sock, brought news of our sister ship. "Apparently," he said, "the electric steering gear's broken down. They've got eight men at the wheel, and they still can't hold her on course."

The prow climbed high into the lurid sky, with foam-flecked fountains spraying the decks, paused as though uncertain of which way to go, swerved, and plunged into a trough between two towering ridges in the roaring seascape. That night, swinging in the hammock, I heard sounds from the galley of the breaking of crockery, the clanging of pots and the slithering of pans—as though a gang of poltergeists were holding a convention. Breakfast next morning wasn't up to par, but the cooks produced a Sunday lunch—turkey and Christmas pudding—of which my mother would have approved. The howl of the gale and the tang of the spray were appetite-enhancing, and I approached every meal with a keenness only briefly blunted when an ill-fitting porthole cover allowed a stream of salty water to splash across the table.

On Monday, although the *Wolfe*'s speed had been reduced to help her keep station, our sister ship was nowhere to be seen. She was somewhere far astern, and the frigate with her. McLeod scanned the horizon, and the approaching snowstorm. "This is jolly good," he said, "all alone in the middle of the ocean. Where's the Navy gone?"

"You might well ask," said Withers. "This area's absolutely thick with U-boats."

Featonby sniffed. "How on earth do you know? You haven't faintest idea where we are."

"I've been working it out, mate, and we're bang in the middle of their killing ground." Excitedly, he pointed at the heaving grayness on the starboard beam. "Look there, for Christ's sake! Isn't that a torpedo, coming straight at us?"

Walker cast a quick glance to his right. "Shut your head, you panicky wee bugger," he said, "or I'll throw you overboard. I'm away below for a game of pontoon."

We played the game by the hour, for a penny a card. That, and ship's duties, were all there was to do. There were so many of us to share out the duties—fatigues, security guard or crewing the Bofors gun—that the chances were against being on the roster more than once. When my turn came around, it was fatigues—humping barrels in the canteen—which wasn't quite so boring as guarding nameless stores against an unknown predator, and a lot less chilling than manning the gun. Withers and I, co-humpers, listened to the rhythmic pounding—like a pneumatic drill working in slow time—as the gunners fired their practice rounds out there in the cold, and agreed that fatigues were not too bad after all.

Next day, the weather was so hostile—"She's shipping the greenies," Burt remarked—that only the duty gun crew were allowed on deck. Down below, the Purser changed our sterling into dollars. "I don't call this money," said McLeod, fingering a note. "We play Monopoly with stuff like this at home."

With nightfall came the sound of heavy gunfire, booming in the distance to the north. No-one told us what it meant—perhaps nobody knew—and it had been forgotten by the time the craggy coast of Nova Scotia appeared on the horizon with the dawn. The *Wolfe* dropped her anchor in Halifax harbour after fourteen days at sea, in the stinging cold of the late afternoon. Its brilliance was fading into twilight as we prepared to disembark.

There was a moment, standing on deck with collar buttoned up and hands deep in pockets, while the shore-lights shone serenely and shimmered on the water, when it truly reached

Images typical of a wartime RAF heavy bomber station in England, as it looked more than forty years after the end of World War II.

The bottom line is that we delivered under extraordinary and unbelievable circumstances.
—Otto Marchica, U.S. Merchant Marine, 1943-50

me that embattled, blacked-out Britain was 2,000 miles away, and that beyond the starlit harbour lay another world. I shuffled down the gangway, with Walker ahead of me, Featonby behind. On the far side of the snow-covered pier, hissing patiently, stood the train that was to take the draft to Moncton in New Brunswick. I stepped across the threshold into North America, slipped on a patch of ice and landed on my back.

On 1st October 1942, with wings on my tunic, a sergeant's chevrons on my sleeve, and 250 flying hours in my log-book, I was standing on the pier at Halifax again. This time, the passage was to take six days, and our ship, the *Stirling Castle*, was sailing in the sort of armada Percy Burt had dreamed of ten months ago at Milford Haven. And it wasn't only the size of the convoy, or its speed, which made the voyage so different from the earlier experience in HMT *Wolfe*. Then, if the draft, as aircrew under training, had gone to the bottom of the Atlantic, only our nearest and dearest would have cared; now, we could fly, and the squadrons needed us. Britain had invested a lot in our training, and was protecting her investment.

No-one slung a hammock aboard the *Stirling Castle*, and someone else did the chores. We slept in bunks and dined in state—as though in a West End restaurant afloat. There was air protection, too.

The long, green sweep of Ireland's coastline looked peaceful and serene in the October sun, as though untouched by war, and it took the sight of Liverpool's disfigurement and Birkenhead's scars to tell us we were home. Everyone on deck was rather quiet as the *Stirling Castle* steamed up the Mersey—quiet, but content. I, for one, had seldom felt so happy. I didn't even fret when I discovered, on the quay, that some light-fingered character had known exactly where to find those little presents for the family, wrapped and ready in a kitbag in the hold. That sort of mishap was just a part of coming home."

The U.S. Liberty ship, *Casimir Pulaski*, had a most interesting mixed cargo: military ambulances on deck and, between decks, Chesterfield cigarettes in one hold, small arms ammunition in another, Dole pineapple juice in another and, finally, phosgene gas in the last hold. This was the only freighter on which I slept with a gas mask suspended over my head. Apparently, the gas was in case the Germans used it first, as they did in WWI. On this ship I saw one of the only two torpedoes that I saw during the war. Had it hit us, I think that the entire convoy would have been wiped out by the gas. An all-welded ship, the *Pulaski*'s welds started to crack just before the centrecastle. They were patched by the ship's carpenter with cement.
—Peter Macdonald, Able Seaman, Canadian Merchant Navy

left: Young and lonely, the simple pleasure of a dance meant a lot to those serving their country far from home.

162

# MALTA

FOR 5,000 YEARS, the Mediterranean has been the arena of great sea battles, and in World War II that historic reputation did not change. When France collapsed in June 1940, the Italian dictator, Benito Mussolini, decided that the time had come when he could, with impunity, join Hitler in the war against the sole remaining member of the Western Allies. From that moment on, the little island of Malta was a highly vulnerable, isolated outpost of the British Empire, and a vital one. Without Malta, the Mediterranean could have been closed to Britain, and her armies in North and East Africa—the only land forces at that time able to engage the enemy—could have been faced with another, and more disastrous, Dunkirk.

The island's excellent harbour of Valetta, well-established airfield, and central position in the mid-east theatre, gave Malta a strategic importance out of all proportion to her size. The problem was that, even more than Britain, Malta needed a constant flow of imports to survive. She had no resources of oil or solid fuel, and very little grain. Even the forage for the goats which supplied the island's milk had to be imported. It was essential for what was to become known as "the classic convoy" to be instituted, and for Malta's reinforcement, code-named Operation Jaguar, to continue for so long as it was needed.

The nearest British bases were Gibraltar, a thousand miles to the west, and Alexandria, almost as distant in the east. The shipping routes from either direction were threatened by the Axis powers' air and sea bases in Sardinia and Tunisia to the west, and from Libya to the east, while Malta herself lay under direct threat from bombers based on Sicily, less than a hundred miles away. Malta's towns and facilities were bombed almost as often as those in south-east England, as were ships in transit and in harbour. The danger from submarines and torpedo boats in the channel between the island of Pantelleria and the Cape Bon peninsula was particularly great, and all the

We were called to boat drill occasionally, which involved donning life-jackets and assembling on the boat deck. We called it 'Board of Trade Sports', and no-one took it very seriously. I can't recall ever seeing the lifeboats swung out when we were at sea, although they were, very occasionally, in port. The old type life-jackets with eight cork blocks were regarded as dangerous because they could break your neck when you jumped into the water. The old hands told us to jump carrying them. The kapol jackets with whistles and lights were a big improvement. It was remarkable that so many seafarers couldn't swim—they used to say 'no-one can swim a thousand miles'.
—Jack Armstrong, tanker steward, Merchant Navy

left: *The Convoy Led by Admiral Vian Fighting its Way Through to Malta, 1942* by Charles Pears

163

more so when, as sometimes happened, the major Royal Navy escort vessels—the battleships, aircraft carriers and heavy cruisers—had to be diverted to fight another battle or meet another threat.

In September 1940, the British Mediterranean Fleet was reinforced by the aircaft carrier HMS *Illustrious*, the battleship HMS *Valiant* and two anti-aircraft cruisers. Furthermore, a squadron of American Martin Maryland aircraft arrived on Malta to carry out reconnaissance flights over Italy. Two months later, Fairey Swordfish aircraft, flying off *Illustrious*, attacked Taranto harbour with bombs and torpedoes, sank three Italian battleships, damaged another, and destroyed the seaplane base. Then, the Germans took a hand. Fliegerkorps X were sent in from Norway with 300 aircraft—Ju-87 Stuka dive-bombers, Ju-88 bombers, Me-110 fighter-bombers and Me-109 fighters; ten U-boats were withdrawn from the Atlantic (to Admiral Dönitz's displeasure) to join the powerful, if variably effective, Italian underwater fleet. On 10th January 1941, Stukas hit *Illustrious* with six 1,000 pound bombs, and put her out of action; a few days later, they did the same to *Furious*. Both carriers had to be withdrawn to America, for repair in Norfolk, Virginia.

Nevertheless, up to the end of 1941, most merchant ships continued to reach Malta safely, but in 1942 the situation changed. Between February and August, of eighty-five merchantmen leaving British ports for Malta, twenty-four were sunk. In June, only two ships out of six that had sailed from the Clyde reached the island, where they were subjected to incessant bombing for the next fifty-four days. Still, the troopers, cargo ships and tankers set out on what was becoming known, not so much as the "classic", but as "the suicide convoy".

In July 1942, a typical single cargo unloaded in the Grand Harbour of Valetta, during what was classified as Operation Tiger, consisted of guns and ammunition, cars and lorries, aviation fuel and spare parts for aircraft, wheat, flour and maize, cement, corned beef, and bales of cloth. The ship which carried that particular cargo was one of nine escorted by the battleship HMS *Nelson*, the aircraft carrier HMS *Ark Royal*, and other warships. Each master in the convoy, before sailing, had received this signal from the escort commander, Vice-Admiral Sir James Somerville:

"For over 12 months Malta has resisted all attacks by the enemy. The gallantry displayed by her garrison and people has aroused admiration throughout the world. To enable this defence to continue it is essential that your ships, with their valuable cargoes, should arrive safely at the Grand Harbour...Remember, everyone, that the watchword is THE CONVOY MUST GO THROUGH."

As usual, the merchant skippers were told that they must not make smoke, that they must not show lights at night, and that, even in daylight, they must only use the dimmest lamps. If their ships were damaged, they must continue sailing at the best speed they could make. On the way to Gibraltar, they had practised evasive action, turning in unison, for two hours at a time, and every gunner had been given the chance to test his armament.

The Rock was blanketed in fog when the convoy navigated the Straits of Gibraltar, and it was as hard for the masters to maintain formation. The navigation lights of the Port Chalmers, carrying 2,000 tons of aviation petrol in four-gallon cans, were switched on at full power, and the *Deucalion*, sailing ahead, showed a cluster of cargo landing lights astern. Two days later, at nine-fifteen in the morning, nine aircraft, thought to be Italian, attacked, but no ship was hit. That evening, however, *Nelson* and *Ark Royal* and *Renown* sped away to the north-east, leaving the cruiser *Edinburgh* and the destroyers to escort the

Do not see danger everywhere and in everything, do not overestimate the enemy, do not always seek to place yourself in his position, do not assume that everything that is going on in the theater of war applies to yourself— these internal reservations and scruples are a sign of uncertainty, and of a negative attitude, which impairs your ability to reach a decision, and endangers the success of the operations.

Audacity and a readiness to take responsibility, coupled with cool, clear thinking, are the pre-conditions and the basis of success.
—from *The U-Boat Commander's Handbook*

Even wartime difficulties did not make me enjoy this method of serving oneself: pick up the tray, slide it along the bars, receive a slop of meat (not too bad, but a bit gristly), far too much potato and gravy and masses of cabbage...The coffee was vile, so I left it.
—from *Mrs Milburn's Diaries: An Englishwoman's Day to Day Reflections* by Peter Donnelly

*right: The tanker 'Ohio' in a Malta Convoy, August 1942 by Norman Wilkinson.*

convoy.

Next day before the sun was up, a fleet of enemy torpedo boats attacked, and the escorting warships' searchlights lit the scene. "We saw an E-boat," said a merchant skipper, "and the cruiser let go with a broadside. When the spray subsided, the E-boat wasn't there." The attacks continued, on and off, for 36 hours, during which time the seamen slept with their clothes on, if they slept at

EVEN THE WALLS--

S'long Dad! We're shiftin' to..
Blimey, I nearly said it!

166

Even in peace, scant quiet is at sea; / In war, each revolution of the screw, Each breath of air that blows the colours free, May be the last life movement known to you.

Death, thrusting up or down, may disunite / Spirit from body, purpose from the hull, / With thunder, bringing leaving of the light, With lightning letting nothingness annul.

No rock, no danger, bears a warning sign, / No lighthouse scatters welcome through the dark; / Above the sea, the bomb; afloat, the mine; / Beneath, the gangs of the torpedo-shark.

Year after year, with insufficient guard, / Often with none, you have adventured thus; / Some, reaching harbour, maimed and battle-scarred, / Some, never more returning, lost to us.

But, if you 'scape, tomorrow, you will steer To peril once again, to bring us bread, / To dare again, beneath the sky of fear, The moon-moved graveyard of your brothers dead.

**overleaf: RAF Spitfires gained air superiority over Malta in spring 1942, right: Loading vital Red Cross food parcels for Allied war prisoners in Germany.**

all, and subsisted on sandwiches and coffee. When they steamed into Valetta, they received the usual enthusiastic welcome from the islanders, crowded on the rocks and ramparts which made the harbour a natural arena, and General Sir William Dobbie, the Governor of Malta, boarded every ship to shake the master's hand. In the fifteen days it took to unload the cargoes into lighters, the harbour was often under air attack, but the seamen stayed aboard their ships. They had brought in 58,000 tons of supplies, without a vessel lost, and were interested to learn, on the radio from Rome, that Mussolini's navy and air force (the Regia Aeronautica) claimed to have sunk a total of 70,000 tons.

That convoy may have been the last to reach Malta more or less intact—at least until May 1943, when the Allied armies drove the enemy out of North Africa. Between February and August 1942, of 85 merchantmen to set out for Malta, 24 were sunk, and 11 had to abort the voyage and return to port. In terms of cargo, 43% of 314,690 tons from Britain, and 34% of 296,000 from Egypt, were lost. Few oil tankers got through in those months, and most of the gasoline was carried by the cargo ships in drums and cans, and once it reached the island it was rapidly dispersed to maximise its survivability.

It was the islanders' steadfastness throughout the summer of 1942, when they were truly under siege, which earned Malta the George Cross—the civilian equivalent of the Victoria Cross. Some of the sharpest action came in August with Operation Pedastel, when a convoy of fourteen ships was two days' sailing eastward from Gibraltar. It included the Port Chalmers, the *Deucalion* and the *Melbourne Star*, all of which had sailed the route in the previous July, and the tanker *Ohio* carrying 11,000 tons of oil. The convoy's escort was of a strength which a merchant skipper on the North Atlantic route would only ever see in dreams. It consisted of the

battleships *Nelson* and *Rodney*, the carriers *Victorious, Eagle, Indomitable* and *Furious* (loaded with Spitfires for Malta's defences), three cruisers, four anti-aircraft cruisers and twenty-four destroyers, with back-up from two oilers, four corvettes, a rescue ship—and all that strength was needed.

Ronald J. Taylor, a Fleet Air Rating on the *Indomitable*, remembers an attack on the carrier by 12 Stuka dive-bombers. "It was frightening," he said, "but you had to admire their skill. Bombs pierced the deck and damaged the hull. I was in the hangar—the coffin, as we called it—when a bomb came down the forward lift. It smashed the twin 4.5 turret on the starboard side, and split the ship from the flight deck to the waterline. Unfortunately a lot of my shipmates were stood against the huge iron doors which enclosed the hangar space, and were crushed when the explosion blew them down. It blew me to the other end of the hangar, then the lift at that end copped it and I was thrown all the way back again. I was wearing steel helmet, flash gear and overalls, and I never had a scratch."

"That was that," continued Taylor. "Our combat air patrols had put up a terrific fight all day, and shot down a lot of enemy aircraft, but now the black balls were out in the signals area, to show we couldn't fly, and we proceeded to damage control and fire-fighting as we turned for Gibraltar. All the way, this great lump that the bombs had torn out of the carrier's side from the bow back 120 feet, was stretching out at right angles and making a terrible noise like an aboriginal 'Didgery-doo'. That was all we could hear until we came into the Straits, and then it was the prisoners-of-war, Italian and German, who were in the holds of ships tied alongside greeting us with shouts of 'Stuka, Stuka, Stuka'. We spent a while putting our casualties on board a trawler for an honourable burial at sea."

On 11th August, a German U-boat, *U73*, hit the aging *Eagle* with four torpedoes, and she heeled

You were salvation to the army lost, / Trapped, but for you, / upon the Dunkirk beach; / Death barred the way to Russia, but you crosst; To Crete and Malta, but you succoured each.

Unrecognised, you put us in your debt; / Unthanked, you enter, or escape, the grave; / Whether your land remember or forget / You saved the land, or died to try to save.
—*For All Seafarers*
by John Masefield

left: A Ju87B Stuka dive bomber, the type led by Major Walter Enneccerus of II/StG2 in a punishing attack on the British aircraft carrier *Illustrious* on 10th January 1941 near the island of Malta. II/StG2 found and sank the cruiser *Southampton* the next day and continued attacks on *Illustrious* in Malta where she was laid up for repairs.

174

over, tipping her equally elderly aircraft overboard. One gallant pilot tried to take off on the sloping deck, but his aircraft slipped into the sea. Within seven minutes, *Eagle* had turned over and gone down. Next day it was the turn of *Indomitable*, from whose deck the Hurricane pilots, waiting to be launched, had watched *Eagle*'s end. Indomitable was hit by bombs, and could no longer launch nor land her aircraft, but those already airborne landed on the flight deck of *Victorious* and continued operating. One merchant vessel had been hit, but she was still afloat.

On that day, 12th August, shortly before the battleships, the cruisers and Indomitable had turned back for Gibraltar, torpedoes from Italian submarines damaged two cruisers and sank an anti-aircraft cruiser. The convoy, with the destroyers and remaining cruisers, keeping close to the coast of Tunisia, sailed on to the south-east, and straight into the sights of the German E-boats. Four merchant ships and a cruiser went down. The Luftwaffe bombers, arriving with the dawn on 13th August, sank another merchant ship and damaged three more, including the *Deucalion*, which later sank. In the course of the day, the tanker *Ohio* was hit by a torpedo and three times by bombs, the third of which stopped her engines.

The *Melbourne Star*, meanwhile, with 4,000 tons of petrol, oil and lubricants aboard, plus 1,450 tons of high explosive, had narrowly avoided a collision during the mêlée when the *Ohio* was first hit. Her master, Captain D.R. MacFarlane, found himself leading the convoy as it passed the lighthouse on Cape Bon. Then, he was overtaken by a destroyer, which led him through the minefields before forging on ahead. Having zig-zagged through a bright shower of shells and tracer bullets, MacFarlane regrouped with the convoy astern of Waiwarama, which was hit by a stick of bombs next morning and blew up. The *Melbourne Star* was showered with debris, and passed through what MacFarlane described as "a sea that was a sheet of fire". Her paintwork was burned away, and the bottoms of her lifeboats were reduced to charcoal. Thirty-six of her crew, seeing death by drowning as a better option than being burned alive, threw themselves into the sea (twenty-two were later rescued by a destroyer and the limping *Ohio*). It was not until she had docked in Valetta that a live six-inch shell was discovered, lodged between the deck planks and the steel ceiling of MacFarlane's day-room. (Sadly, on 2nd April 1943, the *Melbourne Star* was sunk 500 miles south-east of Bermuda by torpedoes from *U129* while carrying a load of ammunition from Australia to Britain via the Panama Canal, and there were only four survivors).

On board the *Ohio*, the crew had somehow got the engines going, and she had rejoined the convoy, steaming at 2 knots, only to have the tail of a shot-down Stuka fall onto her poop deck. Throughout that morning, bombs exploded all around her; she was hit again, a fire broke out, and her engines stopped for good. The fire was partially extinguished, and she was taken in tow by HMS *Rye* with HMS *Penn* and HMS *Ledbury* on either side. With a great hole in her side, her forecastle awash, and fires breaking out from time to time, she was somehow tugged, pushed and jostled for the last twenty miles into Valetta harbour.

The Royal Navy had lost one cruiser, an anti-aircraft ship and a destroyer, with another cruiser and a carrier damaged. Nine merchantmen were down, five the victims of aircraft, four of E-boats, and 350 merchant seamen had been killed. But the cargoes of the four surviving vessels, and *Ohio*'s 11,000 tons of oil, marked the end of the siege of Malta, leading to the breaking of the Axis powers in Africa. Like the island, Captain D.W. Mason, was awarded the George Cross.

On 19th November 1943, the first convoy reached the Grand Harbour unopposed.

We watched a fighter plane attempting to land on a merchant aircraft carrier in bad Atlantic weather. Twice the pilot had to abort, but somehow, on the third attempt, the ship was steady for seconds, and the plane landed just before she pitched and rolled again. We had prayed for that pilot, and our prayers were answered. It was a marvellous sight.
—William Bourner, 2nd Engineer, Merchant Navy

You may be sure we regard Malta as one of the master-keys of the British Empire. We are sure that you are the man to hold it, and we will do everything in human power to give you the means.
—Prime Minister Winston S. Churchill to the Governor of Malta, 6th June 1941

left: Some of the flight deck party of HMS *Victorious* whose pilots fought for two days to save a Malta convoy, 22nd August 1942.

This much is certain; that he that commands the sea is at great liberty, and may take as much and as little of the war as he will.
—Francis Bacon

175

below: One element of the immense D-Day invasion force being brought to shore, right: In what was probably an exercise, HMS *Mauritius*, a Fiji class cruiser, lays a dense smoke screen.

# NORMANDY

overleaf: In April 1944, Southwick Park near Portsmouth became General Eisenhower's operational base. Here the final decision to launch the Normandy invasion was taken, overleaf at bottom: A peaceful Omaha beach in 1994.

Every man in this Allied Command is quick to express his admiration for the loyalty, courage, and fortitude of the officers and men of the Merchant Marine. We count upon their efficiency and their utter devotion to duty as we do our own; they have never failed us yet and in all the struggles yet to come we know that they will never be deterred by any danger, hardship, or privation. When final victory is ours there is no organisation that will share its credit more deservedly

than the Merchant Marine.
—General Dwight D.
Eisenhower, London, June
1944

**D-Day** Any day marking a particularly important event of occasion. The term began to be used during World War I as a code designation for the Allied offensive at Saint-Mihiel. The most famous use of it, however, was in World War II, when it designated the start of the Allied invasion of the Normandy coast. It originally was planned to be June 5, 1944, but was postponed until June 6 owing to bad weather. The "D" has no special significance, simply standing for "day", much as the "H" in H-Hour stands for "hour." However, one writer points out that all amphibious operations have a "departed date," for which D-day may serve as an abbreviation.
—from *Fighting Words* by Christine Ammer

right: Throughout the war, ocean convoys crewed by Allied merchant seamen of many nations brought vital supplies to keep the war effort going. The Normandy D-Day invasion would have been impossible but for their invaluable contribution.

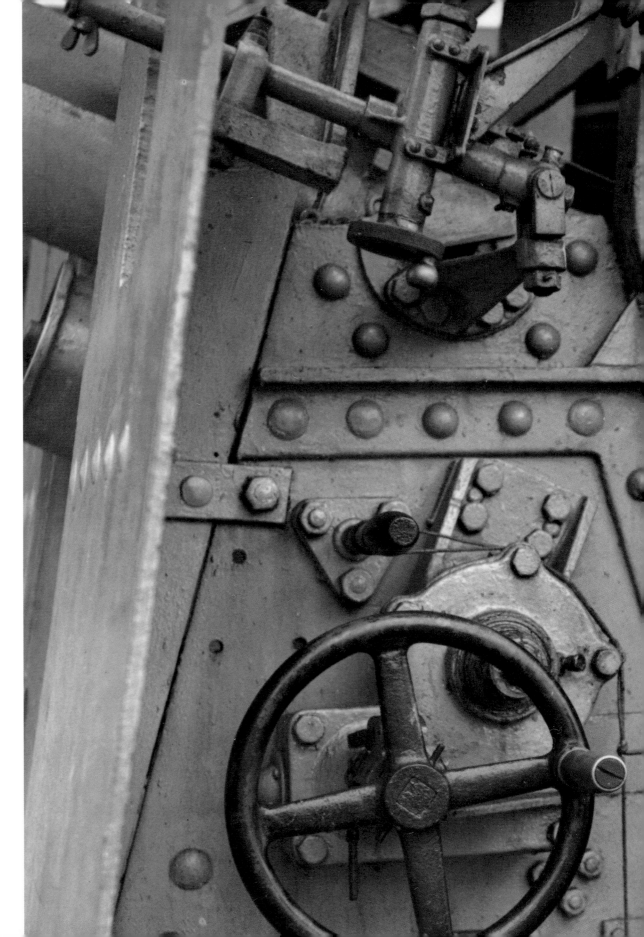

far left: A German gun battery remaining at Longues-sur-Mer, left: Combat equipment of an American padre at Normandy, now on display in the D-Day Museum, Portsmouth, England, below: The remains of the huge Mulberry harbour structures lying off the Arromanches cliffs.

...sailing aboard a liberty offered considerable comfort. The officers' and crew's quarters were all in one house, eliminating the need for men to pass over weather decks to reach messes. Officers were able to retreat to private rooms; crewmen slept two or three to a room. Officers and crew ate at separate sittings, the officers in the "saloon", the crew in another dining area. And one luxury for all were the showers, a great leap forward from the merchant seaman's traditional bucket-washings.
—from *Historic Ships of San Francisco*
by Steven E. Levingston

The gallant Liberty ships brought food, equipment, ammunition, guns and other supplies to the Allied troops in southern England during the run-up to the Normandy Invasion in early 1944. After the landings, the Libertys busily shuttled between England and France, maintaining essential provisions to the beachhead. The *Jeremiah O'Brien* made 11 such supply shuttle trips.

left: The seemingly endless task of repainting a warship, part of keeping her in fighting trim for the demands to come.

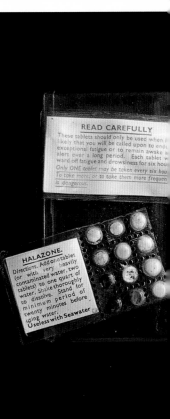

READ CAREFULLY

These tablets should only be used when it is likely that you will be called upon to endure exceptional fatigue or to remain awake and alert over a long period. Each tablet will ward off fatigue and drowsiness for six hours. Only ONE tablet may be taken every six hours. To take more, or to take them more frequently, is dangerous.

HALAZONE.
Directions. Add one tablet (or with very heavily contaminated water, two tablets) to one quart of water; shake thoroughly to dissolve. Stand for minimum period of twenty minutes before using water. Useless with Seawater.

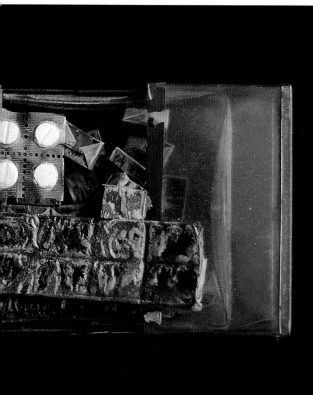

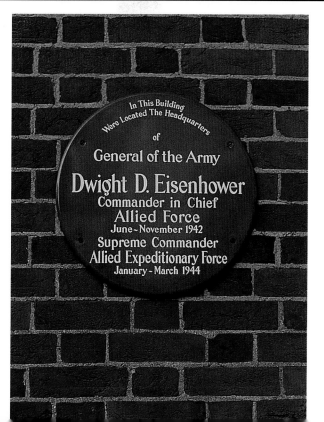

In This Building
Were Located The Headquarters
of
General of the Army
Dwight D. Eisenhower
Commander in Chief
Allied Force
June ~ November 1942
Supreme Commander
Allied Expeditionary Force
January ~ March 1944

above left: The HQ of
Field Marshal Rommel
at Quineville, above
centre: A pillbox near
Pointe du Hoc, above:
Gold beach fronting
Arromanches, far left:
Remnants of the Allied
invasion force at Utah
beach, left centre: 24-
hour type-C survival
rations as used by
airborne troops, left:
Eisenhower's London
headquarters from
January to March 1944.

right: Cramped living
quarters aboard the
typical corvette escort,
above: A merchant
sailor in heavy weather
gear needed in the
days surrounding the
Normandy landings.

far left: Pointe du Hoc, site of the U.S. Army Rangers' cliff assault on German gun batteries. above: Col. James Rudder's men at Pointe du Hoc 6th June 1944.

Technically, destroyers have five different duties. First comes fleet work, for a battle fleet can never go to sea without destroyers as light covering forces. Then there is convoy work. Third comes offensive duties unsupported by bigger ships. Fourth, there is mine laying; and finally, the dozens of odd jobs, such as evacuation. It is a racketing life in destroyers, whether in the North Sea, the Channel, or the Atlantic. Off the East Coast there is never a let-up. The whole art of handling a destroyer successfully consists of seeing the other side first. It is most important, therefore, that glasses (binoculars) should be looked after with the greatest care. If dropped, they will go out of line. Usually they are cherished, and if anyone goes near the captain's glasses there is always likely to be trouble. The hardest job at the start of the war was undoubtedly convoy work. For months at a time individual destroyers would be fourteen days at sea with only forty-eight hours before going out again. They always had steam up, which reflected tremendous credit on the

left: A lookout on watch, overleaf: A Liberation memorial at Oistreham near Caen, and the rusting hulk of an Allied landing craft on Gold beach, Arromanches,

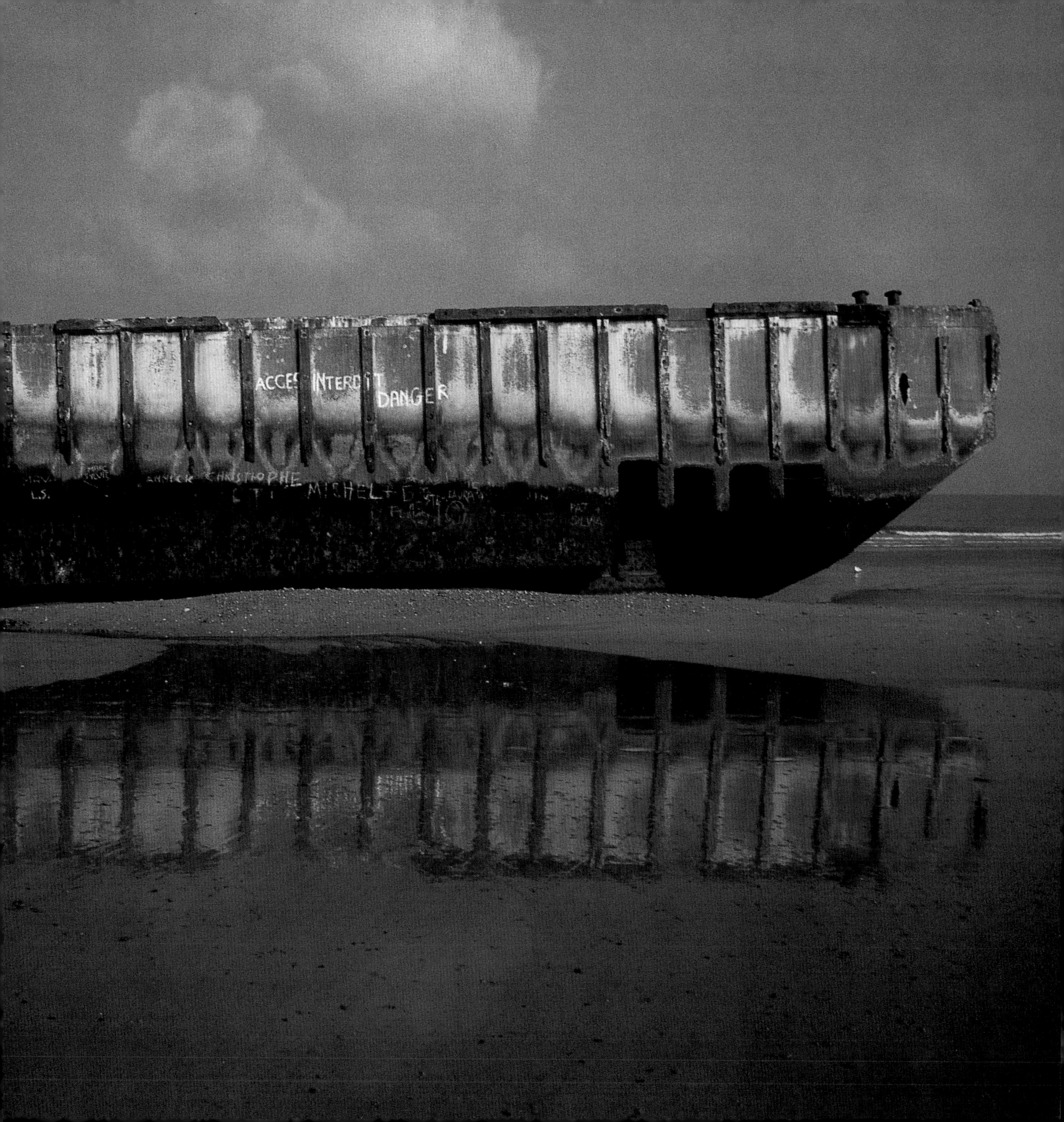
ACCES INTERDIT
DANGER
CHRISTOPHE
MICHEL

engineering side. Stokers
were on watch month in
and month out, and
whereas the upper-deck
crews were able to go on
leave when the destroyer
dropped her hook, the
engine crews had to stay
put.
—from *Life Line*
by Charles Graves

# A CADET'S STORY

*The last two depth charges were not dropped as the buzzers were not working.* This was an extract from my report on an attack on a U-boat. I had a Belgian crew, my report was written in longhand and my Belgian writer who typed it was not familiar with a somewhat similar word. The C.-in-C. Western Approaches must have been rather surprised to read, "The last two depth charges were not dropped as the buggers were not working."
—A.H. Pierce, (C.O.)
HMS *Godetia*

THE SEA CALLED to Peter Guy when he was still a boy at school, and he answered the call as soon as he was old enough—on his sixteenth birthday. He remained a seaman for the next six years and, as it happened, they were the epic years of the Merchant Navy's history. Peter was accepted as a cadet by Lamport & Holt in December 1939, which is where his story starts.

"My first ship was the *Balfe*, and we sailed from Liverpool for the River Plate on 12th January 1940. That winter was severe, and we had barely cleared the Mersey before we ran into a blizzard which lasted some days. It didn't take me long to be seasick, but I still had my watch to keep—four hours on, eight hours off, four hours on and four hours off and so on. I didn't know what I was doing, or what I was supposed to do, but I knew I was cold, wet and miserable. I remember leaving footprints on the snow-covered deck, and with frequent diversions to the side, when I had to go aft to read the log. But I gradually began to get the hang of things, and apart from being sent down to the engine room for the key to the fog locker, and asking the carpenter for a left-handed hammer, I became accepted and started to learn my trade.

*Balfe* was a happy ship with a good master and crew, and in spite of her age, (she was built in 1919), a very good sea boat, as she was to prove some years later. The carpenter was Norwegian, and he gave me two good pieces of advice: get all your drinking and hell-raising done by the age of 21, and always buy the first round when ashore with your shipmates—everyone remembers who bought the first round, but by the fifth or sixth memories begin to be unreliable. He also advised me never to argue with a woman or a wire rope, and how right he was.

Cadets were considered to be the lowest form of marine life, and cheap labour to boot at 15 shillings (75p) per month. All the dirty and unwanted jobs fell to the cadets, but you learned to be a good seaman, and when you became an officer there was no job you would tell a sailor to do that you couldn't do as well, if not better. It was hard work, and sometimes dangerous, and even without overtime we could clock up to 70 hours a week. Entering and leaving port could result in a 12 to 16 hour day.

Our first port was Montevideo, with the *Graf Spee* and her supply ship *Tacoma* very visible. It was strange to see German sailors close up. Then we crossed the estuary of the River Plate to Buenos Aires where, as we had explosives in our cargo, we lay out in the Roads and discharged them into lighters, for which we were paid extra—a welcome addition to the funds, as sixpence (2.5p) a day didn't buy much ashore, even in those days. Argentina was largely pro-German, but we had invitations to various clubs, and at one they had a barbeque where whole oxen and sheep were roasted in trenches.

I was on cargo watching one night, keeping an eye on the stevedores to prevent them broaching the cargo, when one of the firemen came weaving down the quayside. He had been imbibing the local fire-water made from wheat, and as he approached the ship he started hitting the iron bollards, daring them to get up and fight fairly, until his hands were a bloody mess. We got him on board and put him to bed, apparently feeling no pain.

After completing discharge, we set off for Rosario, some 200 miles up the river, where I was introduced to cleaning the bilges (known as bilge-diving); they contained a heady mixture of stinking, stagnant water in which floated putrid and fermenting grain, dead rats and I didn't like to think what else. After a heavy night ashore it was a chastening experience. We loaded a full cargo of bulk and bagged grain and returned safely to Liverpool.

Another job for the cadets was in the chain locker when the anchor was being raised. The locker was steep, narrow and slippery, right up to the bows—

The Battle of the Atlantic was the dominating factor all through the war. Never for one moment could we forget that everything happening elsewhere, on land, at sea, or in the air, depended ultimately on its outcome...Many gallant actions and incredible feats of endurance are recorded, but the deeds of those who perished will never be known. Our merchant seamen displayed their highest qualities, and the brotherhood of the sea was never more strikingly shown than in their determination to defeat the U-boat.
—Winston S. Churchill

Believe me, my young friend, there is *nothing*—absolutely nothing—half so much worth doing as simply messing about in boats.
—from *The Wind in the Willows* by Kenneth Grahame

left: Peter Guy

Opinion is widely held.
*Three senior staff officers agree.*

Under consideration.
*Not under consideration.*

Under active consideration.
*Propose instituting a search for the file.*

Snowed under.
*Only able to take 1 1/2 hours for lunch.*

This will be borne in mind.
*No further action will be taken till you remind me.*

You will remember.
*You have forgotten, if, indeed, you ever knew.*

As you know.
*As you don't know.*

You will appreciate.
*You are far too dense to understand this.*

As your Lordships are well aware.
*My God! We've forgotten to inform the Admiralty.*

right: A wartime convoy conference in progress.

icy in winter and a sweat box in the tropics. You were showered with mud and sea water every time. Nevertheless, I enjoyed my first voyage, and was a very different person from the lad who had set off some three months before.

I rejoined *Balfe* after leave, and we sailed to Southampton, which was to be our base for supplying the BEF in France. Our first trip was to Brest, where we unloaded guns, motor transport and all sorts of supplies, and returned to Southampton, whence we set off again to take our part in the evacuation of Dunkirk. We were either too slow or too late for that, and we were redirected to Cherbourg, where we were convinced that most of the trucks and guns to be brought back were what we had recently discharged at Brest. We loaded as much as possible, but lost the use of the derricks when the soldiers hauled on both the heavy lift guys at the same time, buckled the foremast and put all the cargo gear out of action. We took as many troops on board as we could, and most of them were tired, dispirited and beaten for the moment. They sat or lay down wherever they could, few with any arms or equipment, and we did the best we could for them.

It was at that time we "won" a Bren gun, which made us the best armed ship in our flotilla. Until then, our armament had consisted of two Martini Ross .303 rifles, so the Bren, mounted on Monkey Island, more than doubled our fire power. There were some weird and wonderful ideas on defences early in the war, because of the shortage of weapons. The first "funny" I met was the Holman projector, which consisted of a length of pipe connected by a foot pedal to a compressed air cylinder. A hand grenade, with the pin removed, was put into a tin which just accommodated it and dropped down the pipe. By guess and by God, the pedal was pressed to send the lot flying upwards, with the tin dropping off and the grenade continuing its flight to explode

right in front of the aeroplane and bring it down. However, nobody had thought of putting a gauge on the cylinder to show when the pressure was low, with the result that the tin and grenade would just plop out on the deck, leading to a very hasty exit by all concerned.

An equally daft idea consisted of two rockets, one on each wing of the bridge, connected by a wire with a parachute attached to each. When a plane approached, the rockets would be fired, the parachutes would open at the correct height, with the wire between them, and the plane would obligingly fly into it. There were a few problems: it was impossible to get the rockets to fire at precisely the same time, or to maintain the same rate of climb, even if the wire didn't get snagged in the process. If you got that right, however, and the wire did its job, the liklihood was that the plane would crash onto the ship.

Things got better as the war progressed, and it was quite common to find a ship with a venerable twelve-pounder anti-aircraft gun and a four-inch anti-sub gun of even older vintage. The twelve-pounder had a circular steel emplacement as a protection against strafing, with a high point forward to prevent us shooting up the bridge in an excess of enthusiasm. It was pretty useless, because it took so long to correct the fuse setting and load again after the first shot that the plane was miles away. So we got an improvement: a projector with two rockets on rails that were fired simultaneously by bringing the terminals of a torch battery together. We were all looking forward to seeing it fired, and the great day came when the convoy had dispersed and we were proceeding independently. The gunner, a retired RN Petty Officer, lined everything up, and told us to stand clear while he pressed the terminals together. There was a short period after the rocket ignited, and then whizzed around in a fiery circle. He staggered out of the emplacement with beard and hair singed, and expressed his feelings

far left: Peter Guy in the war years, left: Guy's Merchant Navy identity card.

in a very forceful and moving way. It was most illuminating, in more ways than one.

Balfe's next assignment was to take some 2,000 French servicemen, who didn't want to serve under de Gaulle, to Casablanca, whence they could return to Vichy France. The 'tween decks were made into temporary sleeping/living quarters, and wooden lavatories and cook houses were built on deck. The Germans were in control of the western coast of France, so a long detour into the Atlantic was necessary. We weren't exactly sympathetic to what the French were doing, and our feelings about them were heartily reciprocated (nothing changes). All went well, however; we duly left the French in Casablanca and got away to Gibraltar. That was a strange place then. Nobody knew if Spain would come in on Germany's side, and invade the Rock. It was

decided that women and children, plus males under sixteen and over sixty, were to be evacuated. All merchant ships were pressed into service and we, in view of our previous mission, were well placed to help. We took 500 or so on board and off we went. All went well, and we even had a baby born on board, safely delivered by the Chief Steward, once he had drunk enough whisky to steady his nerves. The baby was named after the Captain and the ship, so somewhere there is a Gibraltarian proudly named Alfred Balfe. We rounded Ireland and delivered our cargo to Swansea. I often wonder what happened to them.

We paid off in the Bristol Channel, and after home leave I joined the Lassell. Alfred Bibby was the master, and Johansen was the carpenter—both from my first voyage in Balfe. Lassell was a lovely ship to sail in, though heavy work on deck with six

After the Normandy landings were over, I joined the Arundel Castle, mostly running prisoners from North Africa to Italy. Then we did an exchange of wounded prisoners, Germans for British POWs, from Marseilles to Göteborg in neutral Sweden. We were granted safe passage, and it was a treat to have portholes open and lights showing. On Christmas Eve 1944, we lay off Gibraltar after embarking the Germans at Marseilles, and everyone who was able gathered on deck to sing a grand selection of carols. I'm sure they were heard in Gibraltar, away in the distance.

Later, we passed through a narrow channel in the Skaggerak into the Baltic, and we could see the faces of the German gunners looking down on us from their gun positions. They weren't very impressed when some of our crew gave them the V-sign. Arriving at Göteborg, we were surprised to get a welcome from a German brass band playing on the quayside. I don't suppose

hatches served by lattice derricks) known as Meccano derricks). She was a twin-screw motor ship, very good in a seaway but difficult to steer, especially in confined waters. We once timed how long it took for the tiller arm to move after the wheel on the bridge was turned, and it was several seconds. A by-product of the steering problem was that one of the cadets (usually me) was put on the wheel when entering or leaving port, which could mean up to six hours of concentrated attention."

Guy's first voyage in *Lassell* was to Bahia, Rio de Janiero and Santos in Brazil, and then, after bunkering in Trinidad, to Boston, Massachusetts. He arrived in time to join the throng in Scollay Square, where everyone was singing, kissing, hugging and seeing in the New Year 1941 in true US fashion. Celebrations over, *Lassell* sailed for Halifax, via the Cape Cod Canal, and, with the convoy Commodore aboard, made the slow journey to Liverpool. It was during an otherwise uneventful trip that one more typical cadet job came Guy's way. It was not too difficult to chip the ice off the officer's toilet outlet while dangling in a bosun's chair: the trick was to rig the chair in such a way that the flood missed him when the blockage was removed.

*Lassell* sailed for South America again on 5th April 1941, with a mixed bulk cargo and a prize bull, destined for breeding in Argentina, penned up on the deck. After a few days, the convoy dispersed, and Captain Bibby headed south, zig-zagging in the daylight until the weather worsened. At 6 o'clock in the evening of 30th April, some 300 miles south-west of the Cape Verdes, Cadet Guy had just completed a two-hour wheel watch, and was looking forward to his dinner, when there was what he described as "an almighty bang". Picking himself up off the deck, he ran to his allotted lifeboat, No. 2, which was on the weather side. The ship was still under way, and the boat was dashed against the side and badly damaged. Cooly, Guy

any other British ship got that in wartime. The saddest part was when close on a hundred of our lads who had lost their sight were led up the gangway. The exchange was all over in about three hours and we sailed home to Liverpool.
—Jack Thompson, cook, *Arundel Castle*

On most of the ships in which I served, the crew's quarters were in the forecastle, the port side allocated to the firemen and the greasers, the starboard side to the seamen, Bosun and carpenter. This varied from ship to ship, with the amount of crew carried. One slept on iron-framed bunks that were constructed one above the lower bunk. Some shipping companies supplied bedding, but to play safe I took a couple of blankets and a mattress with me. These mattresses were made of hessian and filled with straw known as 'a donkey's breakfast', and did not last long before the straw broke down with use and created a lot of dry dust. If you were in the bottom bunk, you were showered with small bits of straw and dust.
—Thomas Rowe, Ordinary Seaman, R.M.S. *Almanzora*

visited his cabin, collected his wallet and a few possessions, and returned to the boat deck to assist in launching the No. 3 boat.

The torpedo, launched from a Type IXB U-boat *U107*, had struck *Lassell* on the port side in the engine room near No. 4 bulkhead. Both engines had stopped, the engine room was flooded, the radio was put out of action, and No. 4 lifeboat was smashed. By ten minutes past six, *Lassell* was settling by the stern as the two remaining lifeboats pulled away. They were followed by a quantity of flotsam, several life-rafts and the bull. Captain Bibby took charge of No. 1 boat, with the 1st and 2nd Officers, 26 men and a lady passenger, while Chief Underhill, in charge of No. 3 boat, had Guy and another 19 men on board. An engineer and a greaser were missing, and they were assumed to have been trapped in the engine room and drowned.

Five minutes later, the U-boat surfaced some 300 yards away from the lifeboats, and members of the crew put an end to the struggles of the bull with their machine guns. Then the U-boat disappeared. In his war diary, Kapitänleutnant Günther Hessler wrote: "Good shot in engine room, large white blast column, ship lists immediately 15 degrees to port, and sinks deeper at the stern. A few seconds after the sinking violent under-water explosions are heard in the submarine."

*Lassell* was Hessler's sixth victim since he set out from Lorient on 29th March. *U107* was re-supplied at sea, and sank another eight merchantmen off the west coast of Africa before completing his patrol, of which, in his memoirs, Admiral Dönitz was to write: "He sank fourteen ships with a total tonnage of 87,000—a remarkable performance... He had already done well on his previous operational tour, and with this recent success added, he had gone well past the success mark at which the award of the Knight's Cross was normally made. But I found it a little difficult to recommend him, because he was my son-in-law.

Eventually the Commander-in-Chief put an end to my hesitations by telling me that if I did not recommend Hessler at once, he would."

As Hessler continued on his deadly way, the men in the boats began to organise themselves. The stores on the wrecked No. 2 boat were removed to No. 3, and Nos. 1 and 3 were balanced by transferring five members of the crew. The radio officer broadcast their position every hour on the portable set. At 6 o'clock in the evening of the second day, a large steamer was sighted, travelling north some four miles to the east. Despite more broadcasts and two distress flares, it continued on its course—a disappointment which was to be repeated several times.

Next morning, a seven-gallon water cask was transferred, to equalise supplies between the boats, and a daily ration was set of three dippers-full per man, for it was clear that the stock of biscuits, corned beef, tinned fruit and condensed milk would outlast the water. It was during that night that the boats lost contact and, despite a show of flashing torches, were unable to regain it. While Chief Officer Underhill in No. 3 boat set a course north-north-east for the Cape Verdes, Captain Bibby aimed further south for Freetown, and it is he who takes up the story at this point.

"After nine days in the boat we were picked up by the *Benvrackie*, and we continued in her until 0830 on 13th May, about 20 miles north of the equator, steering in the direction of Walfish Bay, making about 11 knots and zig-zagging, when she was struck by two torpedoes. The torpedoes struck the engine room and No. 5 hold, and she disappeared in 3 minutes. Only one boat got away, and I was six hours in the water, wearing my life-jacket and hanging on to a piece of wood. There were plenty of sharks around but they kept clear of the wreckage. I was eventually picked up by the boat and found it packed. There were 58 of us in it and no room to move, but it sailed very well, and

During the war, merchant ship engine crews may have had the toughest of all jobs. They could hear the gunfire and feel the explosions, often not knowing when they were in trouble. When their ship was hit, they frequently could not make it up escape ladders or escape trunks (Jacob's ladders hung down the ventilators). These engine crews kept the generators on line to launch boats. Records show that most casualties on the merchant ships were among the engine crews.

One of the great difficulties of protecting ocean-going convoys and independent ships is the limited range of fighter aircraft. Shore-based fighters are ready day and night to take off instantly when word comes of enemy raiders approaching ships in coastal waters, and with their great speed, and with a smoothly working organisation that enables them to locate the menaced ships immediately, they can be on the scene often in time to deal with the enemy. But they have a very limited range. They cannot offer "air cover" at anything like the distance from their bases at which the enemy can threaten ocean-going ships. One of the most ingenious and

below: A merchant ship is torpedoed by a German U-boat.

spectacular devices of the war has been produced to overcome this—the fighter aircraft catapulted from the foredeck of a ship. It is a breathtaking business. The fighter rests in the catapult, ready to be launched. The pilot climbs into the cockpit, starts up his engine, warms it up. He revvs-up, again and again; and then, when he is ready, he gives the signal, and opens the throttle. The aeroplane hurtles off, dipping a little, then zooming up to a steep climb. One moment, the pilot is sitting quietly at his controls, in an aircraft that is quite stationary; the next, he is shooting through the air at nearly a hundred miles an hour, then the sea is just beneath him, and he has to do half a dozen things at once. It takes nerve. It takes coolness, and complete confidence, and a clear brain, and instantaneous thought. These pilots are specially selected for the work. They not only know what they have to do; they know the dangers they run; for they cannot land again on the parent ship. Once in the air, the fighter's job is to get his enemy without thought for himself. When he has done that, he can think about what is to happen to himself. He may be a thousand miles out in the Atlantic. He may have lost

we again made for Freetown.

Half the crew in the boat were Chinese and they were a little troublesome, agitating for more water. They were not rebellious, but as they were accustomed to drinking a lot of water, the ration of half a dipper seemed to worry them. One committed suicide by jumping overboard three times. We pulled him back twice but the third time he got away.

After 13 days in the boat, sailing 500 miles, we were picked up by the hospital ship *Oxfordshire*, which was bound for Freetown. It was dark at the time and we were showing our flares, which were seen on the hospital ship about 7 miles away. Although we were cramped in the small boat and lost the use of our lower legs, we were able to walk up the ladder."

Meanwhile, *Lassells*' No. 3 boat had been sailing south-west by east, as close to the wind as possible, and making two or three knots. With the salvaged stores from No. 2 boat, Chief Officer Underhill's supplies could have lasted for a month. There were ample cigarettes, but a dearth of matches, so when cigarettes were issued after the morning and evening "meals", one match was used to light the first and the rest were lit by mutual ignition, one fag to another. On 6th May it was decided that, with the wind north-east to east-north-east, they were never going to reach the Cape Verde Islands, and that their best course lay east, towards the convoy routes from Freetown—a choice which Captain Bibby had already taken.

On 7th May, the wind dropped, the mainsail was lowered and the oars were manned, but thirty minutes rowing was enough to convince the men that such small progress as was made was not worth the effort. Biscuits, by then, had fallen out of favour as being too thirst-provoking. An alternative seemed to present itself when a squid, holding a flying fish in its tentacles, climbed aboard. So repellent, however, was the creature's

sight of the convoy, and be short of fuel. He may, if fact, have some difficulty in making contact again. If, however, he is within range of an aerodrome where he can land, he makes his own choice whether to attempt to reach it of to be picked up by the convoy. If he decides that he cannot make an aerodrome, there are two courses open to him. He can bring his plane down into the sea near one of the ships, or he can bale out and come down by parachute. In either case, the ship chosed to pick him up must be ready and on the look-out for him. She must know the drill perfectly, for, particularly in stormy seas, it is no easy matter. If the pilot brings his plane down into the water, he will fly low over the ship, passing from stern to bows, and land a short distance ahead. He can then be rescued before the plane sinks. If this is not practicable, he has to bale out, and then he must rely on the ship's captain being able accurately to calculate his drift as he floats down with his parachute, so that the ship will arrive at the spot where he strikes the

overleaf: U-boats in a Biscay drydock, right: Rescue is imminent for the survivors of a torpedoed freighter.

aspect, with eyes bulging from a mottled, reddish head, that it was hurriedly cast back upon the bosom of the deep.

A few men needed medical attention, provided by a steward, for lacerations and abrasions; one suffered from sunburn and another seemed to lose the will to live. On the evening of the 8th May, two men sought permission to hold a short prayer meeting, and this was generally supported. The 2nd Steward led the company in the Lord's Prayer and, after a few moments of silent meditation, a prayer was offered up for urgent rescue—not only for them but for their shipmates in No. 1 boat, whom they had not seen for eight days.

That lonely, heartfelt prayer was answered when daylight broke next morning, as the British liner *Egba* came over the horizon to the west. The company climbed her ladder, all but one without assistance, their sturdy boat was hoisted aboard the after deck, and *Egba* resumed her course for Freetown, passing *Lassell*'s empty No. 1 boat on her way.

When Captain Bibby at last returned to England, he was required to make his report to the Admiralty's casualty section. In concluding it, he recommended that lifeboats should contain fewer biscuits and more water, praised the new kapok life-jackets with red lights and whistles, and commented unfavourably on Freetown's facilities. "It is a very primitive place," he stated, "with little accommodation and an absence of suitable clothing. I would not put a dog in the hotel where I stayed." In this, the Captain was at one with most merchant seamen, who normally referred to the port as Hitler's secret weapon.

In due course, Peter Guy returned to his first ship, the *Balfe*, and remained with her, still as a cadet, still learning seamanship the hard way, while she sailed the oceans of the world. At last, returning to London from another voyage to

water almost as soon as he does so. In either case, it means a very cold bath—and a very risky one. But these catapult-fighter pilots take it all as a matter of course.
—from *The Merchant Service Fights Back* by Wilson MacArthur

"Only numbers can annihilate," said Nelson; and he spoke of ships, not men. The Admiralty would have done well to have borne that saying in mind. After a war, England is very like a dog who has been flung into the sea: when she emerges, panting and exhausted, she shakes herself, wags her tail and proceeds to forget her unwelcome experience. So it was that in the years which succeeded the Peace Conference she forgot the lessons she had learned in bitter suffering, and divested herself of her sea power, first by leading the way in disarmament, then by granting Germany freedom to build a new navy, and finally by relinquishing any claim to her naval bases in Eire.
—from *Red Ensign* by Owen Rutter

South America, he discovered that he had enough sea-time to qualify for a 2nd Mate's ticket—provided he could pass the examinations. The trouble was that, as he said "I had never held a sextant or done any navigational work whatsoever, so I had to start from scratch." That meant a course of study at Sir John Cass College in London, and Lamport & Holt only paid a man for time at sea. It meant the dole for Guy, and luckily a billet near the College with a kindly aunt.

"There were a number of others like me, having to learn and work hard to do so. One day, during a coffee break, a naval officer came in. He said he was from the Admiralty, looking for keen, dashing young men to serve as navigation officers on destroyers, corvettes and the like. A number of us were attracted by the idea, and he went on to explain that first we had to get out of the Merchant Navy (a reserved occupation) and the way to do that was to volunteer for submarines, and that once we were in the RN, he would ensure that we got into escort vessels. A few days later, an RAF officer came in, and told us that when he was at John Cass studying for his ticket like us a naval officer had arrived with just such an offer, but with the difference that first he had to volunteer to be an RAF navigator. He had done that, and ever since he had been sitting over Berlin being fired at by all and sundry, and nursing a dream of meeting a certain naval officer in a dark alley somewhere."

All such snares and delusions avoided, Guy obtained his certificate. He returned to Lamport & Holt as 2nd Mate of the *Samarovsk*, and plied between Antwerp and Tilbury with war stores for the Allied armies until the war was won. Then it was marriage to his Wren sweetheart, and a decision that the time had come for him to swallow the anchor. It was a measure of how far he had travelled in the last six years that when he made one more voyage aboard his first ship, he found himself thinking of her as "the dear old *Balfe*".

A Brief Marine
Terminology Guide

ABAFT: behind; toward stern.

ABEAM: at right angles to the keel.

AMIDSHIPS: the middle portion of a vessel.

ARMOR: steel plating designed to defeat shells, bombs or underwater explosion.

ARMOR BELT: band of armor extending along a ship's sides above and below the water-line.

ATHWART: across; from side to side; transversely.

BEAM: extreme width of ship.

BILGE: curved part of ship's hull where sides and flat bottom meet.

BLISTER: a bulge built into a ship's side as a protection against torpedoes.

BOOM: a free-swinging spar used to secure boats or to handle cargo, boats or aircraft.

BREAK: the point at which upper decks are discontinued.

BRIDGE: raised forward platform from which ship is conned and navigated.

BULKHEAD: transverse of longitudinal partitions sub-dividing the interior of a ship.

BULWARKS: light plating or wooden extension of ship's sides above upper deck.

CASEMATE: armored gun mount built into the sides or superstructure of a ship.

CLASS: vessels of the same

## PICTURE CREDITS

Photographs by Philip Kaplan are credited: PK. Photos from the author's collections are credited: AC. Jacket front: John Hamilton-Imperial War Museum; jacket back: PK. Jacket back flap: Philip Kaplan: Margaret Kaplan; Jack Currie: PK. PP2-3: PK, PP6-7: E.D. Walker, P8: Public Archives of Canada, P10 both: Peter Wakker, P11: AC, PP12-13: Canadian Forces, P14: PK, P15 left and centre: Vera Dunnett; right: PK, P17: Imperial War Museum, P18: National Maritime Museum, P19 top: Imperial War Museum, bottom: Public Archives of Nova Scotia, P20 both: Public Archives of Nova Scotia, PP22-23: Thomas Harold Beament-Canadian War Museum, P24: Public Archives of Nova Scotia, P25: Public Archives of Nova Scotia, P26: Michael O'Leary collection, P27: Public Archives of Nova Scotia, P28: Imperial War Museum, P29: Imperial War Museum, P30: Jack Armstrong, P31: Jack Armstrong, P32: Public Archives of Nova Scotia, P33: Imperial War Museum, P34: Stephen Bone-National Maritime Museum, P35: Michael O'Leary collection, P36: both: Bundesarchiv, P37: Bundesarchiv, P38 left: Bundesarchiv; right: Adolph Bock-US Army Art Collection, P39 top left: Bundesarchiv; top right and bottom: PK, P40: National Archives of Canada, P41: Canadian Forces, P42: Norman Wilkinson-National Maritime Museum, P43: Michael O'Leary collection, P44: San Diego Aerospace Museum, P45: San Diego Aerospace Museum, P46 top: AC; bottom: Anne Turley-George, P47: National Archives, P49: Imperial War Museum, P50: Richard Eurich-Imperial War Museum, P53 all: Jack Thompson, P54: AC, P55: AC, P56: AC, P57: Imperial War Museum, P58 top both: Michael O'Leary collection, P59 all: Michael O'Leary collection, P60: National Archives, P61: Bundesarchiv, P62: AC, P63: AC, P64: Imperial War Museum, PP66-67 all: PK, P68: The National Liberty Ship Memorial, P70 top: Michael O'Leary collection; bottom both: AC, P71: AC, P72: British Film Institute, P73: AC, PP74-75 all: PK, P76 both: AC, P77: National Archives of Canada, P78: Norman Wilkinson-Canadian War Museum, P79: Bill Hudson, P80: AC, P81: Imperial War Museum, P82: Norman Wilkinson-Canadian War Museum, P83: PK, P84 both: Bundesarchiv, P85: Bundesarchiv, P86 top: Bundesarchiv; bottom: PK, P87: AC, P88: Canadian Forces, P89 all: AC, P90: AC, P91 both: Imperial War Museum, P93: Public Archives of Nova Scotia, P94: US Coast Guard, P96: AC, P98: Franc Isla collection, P99 top both: AC; bottom: Thomas Harold Beament-Canadian War Museum, P100 both: AC, P102 left: William Bourner; right: AC, P103: AC, P104: AC, P106: Imperial War Museum, P107: Thomas Harold Beament-Canadian War Museum, P109: Canadian Forces, P110: Imperial War Museum, P111: Felix Topolski-Imperial War Museum, P112 left: Robert Atkinson; right: R.S.Snell, P113: Maritime Museum of the Atlantic, P114: Thomas Harold Beament-Canadian War Museum, PP116-117 both: Public Archives of Nova Scotia, P118: AC, P119 top: Charles Bishop; bottom: AC, P121: Felix Topolski-Imperial War Museum, P122: Norman Wilkinson-National Maritime Museum, P123: Michael O'Leary collection, P124: AC, P125: British Film Institute, P126: Geoffrey Spink Bagley-Canadian War Museum (every effort was made to find the copyright holder), P127 all: PK, P128 bottom left: A.H. Pierce, P129 far right: British Film Institute; all other photos: AC, P130 far left: Cyril Hatton; all other photos: PK, P131 top: Thomas Charles Wood-Canadian War Museum; bottom: PK, P132: National Archives of Canada, P133: Robert Seager, P134 left both: Jack Belcher, P135: Donald Cameron Mackay-Canadian War Museum, PP137: AC, P139: John Hamilton-Imperial War Museum, P140: Public Archives of Nova Scotia, P143: Alex Colville-Canadian War Museum, P146: Thomas Charles Wood-Canadian War Museum, P149: Imperial War Museum, P151: Canadian Forces, P152: Jack Currie, P154: Michael O'Leary, P155: Imperial War Museum, P157: National Archives of Canada, PP158-159 all: PK, P160: Public Archives of Nova Scotia, P162: Charles Pears-Imperial War Museum, P164: Imperial War Museum, P166: AC, P167: Norman Wilkinson-Imperial War Museum, PP168-169: Michael O'Leary, P171: American Red Cross, P172: Bundesarchiv, P174: Imperial War Museum, P176: Lt. G. Milne, RCNVR-Canadian Forces, P177: AC, P178: Royal Navy, P179 both: PK, P181: Imperial War Museum, PP182-183 all: PK, PP184-185: National Archives of Canada, PP186-187 all: PK, P188: AC, P189: Maritime Museum of British Columbia, P190: PK, P191: AC, P192: Imperial War Museum, PP194-195 both: PK, PP196-197: Imperial War Museum, P198: Peter Guy, P201: AC, P202: Peter Guy, P203: Peter Guy, P204: Imperial War Museum, P206: Imperial War Museum, PP207-208: Bundesarchiv, P211: Bundesarchiv, P213: Imperial War Museum, P215: Canadian Forces, P216: Imperial War Museum, P218: E.D. Walker, P220: National Archives of Canada.

## ACKNOWLEDGEMENTS

The authors thank the following people for their help with this book: Jack Armstrong, John Atwood, Geoff Barlow, H. Battersby, William Beacham, Jack Belcher, Charles Bishop, Quentin Bland, William Bourner, Clive Brookes, Piers Burnett, Tony Cooper, Kate Currie, Hargita Danko, William C. Dawson, Vera Dunnett, Francis Flaherty, Ella and Oz Freire, Samuel F. Glyn, Marilyn Gurney, Peter Guy, H.G. Hall, Cyril Hatton, Thom Hendrickson, Lord Geoffrey Howe, Bill Hudson, Franc Isla, Claire Kaplan, Margaret Kaplan, Neal Kaplan, The U.S. National Liberty Ship Memorial-S.S. *Jeremiah O'Brien*, Grant Lucas, Keith MacArthur, Otto Marchica, Bill McCreadie, Judy and Rick McCutcheon, Morris McGaffney-HMCS *Sackville*, Tilly and James McMaster, Norman Meyer, Thomas Nash, William Newman, Lynn and Michael O'Leary, Sir John Palmer, A.H. Pierce, Kathleen Pollard, C.H. Rayner, Lynn Richard, Tom Rowe, Robert Seager, Ronald S. Snell, Cyril J. Stephens, Ian Stockbridge, Jack Thompson, E.D. Walker, Peter Wakker, G. Watson, Bill Wilson and E. Withers. Excerpts and other material from *Finished With Engines* printed with the kind permission of Robert Richard Atkinson.

type built to a common basic design.

COMBINED OPERATIONS: joint operations conducted by nonhomogeneous forces or forces of different services and/or nationalities.

COMPANIONWAY: hatchway providing access from one deck to another.

COMPARTMENTATION: subdivision of a ship's hull by means of transverse and/or longitudinal bulkheads.

CONNING TOWER: armored ship control station. In submarines, the main deck structure.

COUNTER: side of a vessel's quarter.

COWL: a smoke baffle located on top of a funnel; opeing of a ventilator.

DAMAGE CONTROL: comprehensive term for all means of mitigating or offsetting effects of damage aboard ship.

DEPTH CHARGE: explosive device projected or dropped from air or surface craft; detonated at predetermined depths by a hydrostatic mechanism.

DISPLACEMENT: the weight of water displaced by a ship.

FANTAIL: after section of the main deck.

FORE: that part of a ship lying between bow and midship section.

FORE AND AFT: lengthwise of a ship.

FORECASTLE: deck; a forward upper deck extending to bow.

E. D. WALKER

## BIBLIOGRAPHY

Bailey, Chris H., *The Battle of the Atlantic, The Corvettes and their Crews: An Oral History*, Alan Sutton Publishing Ltd, 1994.

Beaver, Paul, *U-Boats in the Atlantic*, Patrick Stephens Ltd, 1979.

Bekker, Cajus, *The German Navy 1939-1945*, Dial Press, 1974.

Botting, Douglas, *The U-Boats*, Time-Life Books—The Seafarers, 1979.

Breyer, Siegfried, & Koop, Gerhard, *The German Navy at War 1939-45*, Schiffer.

Brookes, Ewart, *The Gates of Hell*, Arrow Books, 1973.

Broome, Jack, *Convoy Is To Scatter*, William Kimber, 1972.

Buchheim, Lothar-Günther, *U-Boat War*, Bantam Books, 1978.

Cameron, Ian, *Red Duster, White Ensign*, White Lion, 1974.

Cantwell, John C., *Images of War—British Posters 1939-45*, HMSO.

Clancy, Tom, *Submarine*, Berkley Books, 1993.

Costello, John, & Hughes, Terry, *The Battle of the Atlantic*, Fontana-Collins, 1977.

Course, *The Merchant Navy Today*, Oxford University Press, 1956.

Cremer, Peter, *U-Boat Commander*, Naval Institute Press, 1985.

Crowther, J.G., & Whiddington, R., *Science At War*, HMSO, 1947.

De Launay, J., & De Schutter, J., *Arromanches 44 The Normandy Invasion*, Editions J.M. Collet, 1984.

Desquesnes, Rémy, *Normandy 1944*, Editions Ouest-France Memorial De Caen, 1993.

Dönitz, Karl, *Memoirs*, Greenhill Books, 1990.

Dyer, Jim & Edwards, Bernard, *Death and Donkey's Breakfasts*, D & E Books.

Edwards, Bernard, *The Merchant Navy Goes To War*, Robert Hale, 1990.

Edwards, Bernard, *Under Four Flags*, Percival

FREEBOARD: height of a ship's sides from water-line to a weather deck.

FLYING BRIDGE: a light self-supporting structure extending from side of ship's bridge.

GUN HOUSE: a lightly protected, rotating mount for guns of lesser calibre.

GUN SHIELD: any protection for gun crews which does not completely enclose mount.

GUNWALE: upper edge of a vessel's or boat's side.

HALYARDS: light lines used in hoisting signals, flags, etc.

HATCH: opening in a deck.

HELM: the mechanism for operating the ship's rudder.

HULL: main body of a vessel exclusive of elements of superstructure.

ISLAND: a free-standing section of a ship's superstructure. On aircraft carriers, the ship's superstructure.

KEEL: center line strength member running fore and aft along the bottom of a ship.

KNOT: a unit of speed, equalling one nautical mile per hour.

LIST: transverse inclination of a vessel.

MAIN BATTERY: the heaviest calibre gun armament carried by a naval vessel.

MAIN DECK: a ship's highest continous deck.

MINE: a device containing high explosive charge, free-

previous spread: *Atlantic Convoy* by E.D. Walker, right: At the Merchant Navy Memorial, Tower Hill, London.

floating or anchored at fixed depth, or resting on bottom; detonated by contact, or by electrical or magnetic impulse.

MULTIPLE MAST: an exposed mast having one or more supporting elements.

PEAK (fore and aft): compartment at the extreme bow or stern of vessel below decks—usually a tank.

PORT: left-hand side of a vessel when looking towards the bow; an opening.

QUARTER: that portion of a vessel's side near the stern.

QUARTER DECK: part of upper deck reserved for officers; also the deck near the stern.

RADIO DIRECTION FINDER: device for determining direction of source of radio impulses.

RAKE: fore and aft inclination from vertical.

RANGEFINDER: optical instrument for determining distance to a target or other object.

RECIPROCATING ENGINE: a steam-actuated piston engine as distinguished from a turbine.

RIGGING: collective term for ropes and chains

Marshall, 1954.

Farrago, Ladislas, *The Tenth Fleet*, Drum Books, 1962.

Frank, Wolfgang, *The Sea Wolves*, Mann, 1973.

Gallery, Daniel V., *Twenty Million Tons Under The Sea,* Regnery, 1956.

Gannon, Michael, *Operation Drumbeat*, Harper Perennial, 1990.

Giese, Otto, *Shooting The War*, Naval Institute Press, 1994.

Graves, Charles, *Life Line*, William Heinemann.

Gray, Edwin, *The Killing Time*, Scribners, 1972.

Gretton, Sir Peter, *Crisis Convoy*, P. Davies, 1974.

Hadley, Michael, *Count Not The Dead*, Naval Institute Press, 1995.

HMSO, *Ark Royal*.

HMSO, *The Battle of the Atlantic*, 1946.

HMSO, *Coastal Command*, 1942.

HMSO, *East of Malta, West of Suez*, 1943.

HMSO, *Merchantmen At War*.

HMSO, *The U-Boat War in the Atlantic 1939-45*.

Hurd, Sir Achibald, *The Battle of the Seas*, Hodder & Stoughton.

Jaffe, Walter W., *The Last Liberty: The Biography of the SS Jeremiah O'Brien*, Glencannon Press.

John Jahr Verlag, *Waffen im Einsatz*, 1976.

Jones, Geoffrey, *Defeat of the Wolf Packs*, William Kimber, 1986.

Jones, Geoffrey, *Submarines Versus U-Boats*, William Kimber, 1986.

Kemp, Paul, *Convoy Protection*, Arms & Armour, 1993.

Kemp, Peter, *Decision At Sea: The Convoy Escorts*, Elsevier-Dutton.

Knox, Collie, *Atlantic Battle*, Methuen & Company, 1941.

Lamb, Charles, *To War in a Stringbag*, Nelson Doubleday, 1977.

Lewin, Ronald, *Ultra Goes To War,* McGraw-Hill, 1978.

Levingston, Steven E., *Historic Ships of San Francisco,* 1984.

Lund, Paul, & Ludham, Harry, *Night of the U-Boats,* New English Library, 1974.

Lynch, Thomas G., *Canada's Flowers: History of the the Corvettes of Canada 1939-1945,* 1981.

Macbeth, Jack, *Ready, Aye, Ready*, Key Porter Books, 1989.

Macintyre, Donald, *The Battle of the Atlantic*, Pan Books, 1961.

Macintyre, Donald, *The Naval War Against Hitler*, Batsford, 1971.

Macpherson, Ken, & Milner, Marc, *Corvettes of the Royal Canadian Navy 1939-1945,* Vanwell Publishing, 1993.

Margolin, V., *Propaganda: Persuasion in WWII Art*, Chelsea House, 1976.

Mason, David, *U-Boat: The Secret Menace*, Ballantine Books, 1968.

McKee, Alexander, *The Coal-Scuttle Brigade*, New English Library, 1973.

Messenger, Charles, *World War II in the Atlantic*, Warfare Books and Toys Ltd., 1990.

Metson, Graham, *An East Coast Port...Halifax At War 1939-1945,* McGraw-Hill Ryerson, 1981.

Middlebrook, Martin, *Convoy*, Penguin Books, 1978.

Monsarrat, Nicholas, *Three Corvettes*, Mayflower, 1972.

Morison, Samuel Eliot, *The Battle of the Atlantic*, Volume One, Little Brown, 1947.

Mulligan, Thomas P., *Lone Wolf-Werner Henke*, Praeger, 1993.

Parker, Mike, *Running The Gauntlet,* Nimbus Publishing, 1994.

Pitt, Barrie, *The Battle of the Atlantic*, Time-Life Books, 1977.

Poolman, Kenneth, *The Catafighters and Merchant Aircraft Carriers,* William Kimber, 1970.

Poolman, Kenneth, *Escort Carrier, 1941-1945*, Shepperton, 1972.

Preston, Anthony, *Flower Class Corvettes*, Bivouac Books, 1973.

Rasmussen, Henry, *D-Day Plus Fifty Years*, Top Ten Publishing, 1994.

Robertson, Terence, *The Golden Horseshoe*, Evans Brothers, 1955.

Rogers, Stanley, *Sailors At War*, George G. Harrap.

Rossler, Eberhard, *The U-Boat*, Naval Institute Press, 1989.

Runyan, Timothy, & Copes, Jan M., *To Die Gallantly,* Westview Press, 1994.

Rutter, Owen, *Red Ensign*, Robert Hale.

Schofield, B.B., *Operation Neptune*, Allan, 1974.

Schofield, B.B., *The Russian Convoys*, B.T. Batsford, 1964.

Shaw, Frank H., *The Merchant Navy At War*.

Shea, M., *Maritime England-The Nation's Heritage*, *Country Life* Books, 1981.

Showell, J.P. Malmann, *The German Navy in World War Two*, Naval Institute Press, 1991.

Showell, J.P. Malmann, *U-Boats Under the Swastika,* Naval Institute Press, 1989.

Smith, P.C., *Arctic Victory*, Kimber, 1975.

Smith, P.C., *Pedestal-The Malta Convoy of August 1942,* Crecy Books, 1994.

Syrett, David, *The Defeat of the German U-Boats*, University of South Carolina, 1994.

Tarrant, V. E., *The U-Boat Offensive 1914-1945*, Naval Institute Press, 1989.

*The U-Boat Commander's Handbook*, Thomas Publications, 1989.

Vause, Jordan, *U-Boat Ace: Wolfgang Lüth*, Naval Insitute Press, 1976.

Warlimont, Walter, *Inside Hitler's Headquarters 1939-1945,* Presidio Press, 1993.

Waters, John M., *Bloody Winter*, Naval Insitute Press, 1967.

Werner, Herbert A., *Iron Coffins*, Holt, Rinehart & Winston, 1969.

Westwood, David, *The Type VII U-Boat*, Naval Insitute Press, 1984.

Willans, Geoffrey, *One Eye On The Clock*, Macmillan & Company.

Winterbotham, F.W., *The Ultra Secret*, Futura Publications, 1976.

Winton, John, *Ultra At Sea*, Leo Cooper, 1988.

The authors wish to thank the following people whose quotations appear in *Convoy*: Christine Ammer, Jack Armstrong, Brooks Atkinson, Robert Atkinson, Francis Bacon, J. J. Banigan, Charles Bishop, Elizabeth Bishop, William Bourner, Samuel Butler, George Gordon Lord Byron, Winston S. Churchill, William J. Clinton, Samuel T. Coleridge, Joseph Conrad, Peter Donnelly, Dwight D. Eisenhower, Joseph Fabry, The Falkirk *Herald*, James E. Flecker, Sir Humphrey Gilbert, W.S. Gilbert, Kenneth Grahame, Charles Graves, Peter Guy, H.G. Hall, Cyril Hatton, Thom Hendrickson, Charles Hill of Bristol—Shipbuilders, Samuel Johnson, Ernest J. King, Rudyard Kipling, Collie Knox, Frank Knox, John Lester, Steven E. Levingston, Peter Lewis, Peter MacDonald, Otto Marchica, Edwin Markham, John Masefield, Wilson McArthur, Nicholas Monsarrat, Eugene O'Neill, Sir John Palmer, A. H. Pierce, C. H. Rayner, Phil Richards, Francis Rockwell, S. Roskill, Thomas Rowe, Owen Rutter, Carl Sandburg, Leonard Sawyer, William Shakespeare, Frank H. Shaw, Neil Thomson, Harry S. Truman, Nancy Byrd Turner, Jack Thompson, Peter Wakker, Herbert Werner, Robert Westall, W. Whiting, J. W. S. Wilson, Woodrow Wilson, Roger P. Wise and E. Withers.

employed to support masts, yards, and booms of vessel.

SHEER: longitudinal upward or downward curvature of deck or gunwale.

SHEER LINE: line formed by intersection of deck and sides of a ship.

SPLINTER SCREEN: light armor shields for protection of crew.

STACK: exposed uptake from ship's boilers; funnel.

STARBOARD: the right-hand side of a vessel when looking towards the bow.

STEM: extreme forward line of bow.

STERN POST: the main vertical post in the stern frame upon which the rudder is hung.

SUPERSTRUCTURE: any structure built above a ship's hull.

TASK FORCE: a naval force organised to carry out a specific mission.

TURRET: a rotating mount enclosed by armor for guns of large calibre.

TWIN TURRET: a turret housing two guns.

TYPE: all vessels built or converted for the same purpose.

WEATHER DECK: any deck exposed to weather.

WELL: a lateral opening in a ship's hull or superstructure.

# INDEX